CIMA

EXAM PRACTICE KIT

STRATEGIC LEVEL

PAPER E3

STRATEGIC MANAGEMENT

FOR EXAMS IN 2017

BPP
LEARNING MEDIA

Third edition 2016

ISBN 9781 5097 0702 7
e-ISBN 9781 5097 0735 5

British Library Cataloguing-in-Publication Data
A catalogue record for this book
is available from the British Library

Published by

BPP Learning Media Ltd
BPP House, Aldine Place, 142/144 Uxbridge Road
London W12 8AA

www.bpp.com/learningmedia

Printed in the United Kingdom by

Wheatons Exeter Ltd
Hennock Road
Marsh Barton
Exeter
EX2 8RP

Contents

Question and Answer index

Using your BPP Exam Practice Kit

One of the key criteria for achieving exam success is question practice. There is generally a direct correlation between candidates who study all topics and practise exam questions and those who are successful in their real exams. This Kit gives you ample opportunity for such practice throughout your preparations for your OT exam.

All questions in your exam are compulsory and all the component learning outcomes will be examined, so you must **study the whole syllabus**. Selective studying will limit the number of questions you can answer and hence reduce your chances of passing. It is better to go into the exam knowing a reasonable amount about most of the syllabus rather than concentrating on a few topics to the exclusion of the rest.

Practising as many exam-style questions as possible will be the key to passing this exam. You must do questions under **timed conditions**.

Breadth of question coverage

Questions will cover the whole of the syllabus so you must study all the topics in the syllabus.

The weightings in the table below indicate the approximate proportion of study time you should spend on each topic, and are related to the number of questions per syllabus area in the exam.

E3 Strategic Management Syllabus topics	Weighting
A Interacting with the organisation's environment	20%
B Evaluating strategic position and strategic options	30%
C Leading change	20%
D Implementing strategy	15%
E The role of information systems in organisational strategy	15%

The Objective Test (OT) exam

The OT exam is a computer based assessment, which is available on demand at assessment centres all year round.

OT exams in each level can be taken in any order, but candidates must pass all the OT exams for a level before they can sit the Integrated Case Study Exam for that level.

Each exam lasts for 90 minutes and the pass mark is 70%.

Results are available shortly after the test has been completed, and the results will include feedback.

The exam will be made up of different types of questions, including: -

Question Type	Explanation
Multiple choice	Standard multiple choice items provide four options. 1 option is correct and the other 3 are incorrect. Incorrect options will be plausible, so you should expect to have to use detailed, syllabus-specific knowledge to identify the correct answer rather than relying on common sense.
Multiple response	A multiple response item is similar to a multiple choice question, except that more than one response is required. You will normally (but not always) be told how many options you need to select.
Drag and drop	Drag and drop questions require you to drag a "token" onto a pre-defined area. These tokens can be images or text. This type of question is effective at testing the order of events, labelling a diagram or linking events to outcomes.
Gap fill	Gap fill (or "fill in the blank") questions require you to type a short numerical response. You should carefully follow the instructions in the question in terms of how to type your answer – eg the correct number of decimal places.
Hot spot	These questions require you to identify an area or location on an image by clicking on it. This is commonly used to identify a specific point on a graph or diagram.
Drop-down list	Drop-down lists follow the same principle as multiple choice questions, in that you need to select one option from a pre-defined list. This can be used in conjunction with a gap-fill question: for example, you may be asked to key a numerical answer into a gap-fill box and then select an explanation for the approach you've taken from a drop-down list.

Learning Objectives

The table below has been prepared by CIMA to help you understand the abilities that CIMA is seeking to assess.

Learning objective	Verbs used	Definition	Example question types
1 Knowledge			
What you are expected to know	• List	• Make a list of	MCQ
	• State	• Express, fully or clearly, the details of/facts of	MCQ
	• Define	• Give the exact meaning of	MCQ
2 Comprehension			
What you are expected to know	• Describe	• Communicate the key features of	Multiple Response
	• Distinguish	• Highlight the differences between	Multiple Response
	• Explain	• Make clear or intelligible/state the meaning or purpose of	Drop down list
	• Identify	• Recognise, establish or select after consideration	Hotspot
	• Illustrate	• Use an example to describe or explain something	Drop down list
3 Application			
How you are expected to apply your knowledge	• Apply	• Put to practical use	Multiple response
	• Calculate/ compute	• Ascertain or reckon mathematically	Number entry
	• Demonstrate	• Prove the certainty or exhibit by practical means	Hotspot
	• Prepare	• Make or get ready for use	Drag and drop
	• Reconcile	• Make or prove consistent/ compatible	Drop down list
	• Solve	• Find an answer to	Number entry
	• Tabulate	• Arrange in a table	Drag and drop
4 Analysis			
How you are expected to analyse the detail of what you have learned	• Analyse	• Examine in detail the structure of	Multiple response
	• Categorise	• Place into a defined class or division	Drag and drop
	• Compare & contrast	• Show the similarities and/or differences between	Hotspot
	• Construct	• Build up or complete	Drag and drop
	• Discuss	• Examine in detail by argument	Multiple response
	• Interpret	• Translate into intelligible or familiar terms	Multiple response
	• Prioritise	• Place in order of priority or sequence for action	Drop down list
	• Produce	• Create or bring into existence	Drag and drop

Learning objective	Verbs used	Definition	Example question types
5 Evaluation			
How you are expected to use your learning to evaluate, make decisions or recommendations	• Advise	• Counsel, inform or notify	Multiple response
	• Evaluate	• Appraise or assess the value of	Multiple response
	• Recommend	• Propose a course of action	Multiple response

In your CBA, questions will be set which test up to the cognitive level of the verb in the component learning outcome in each paper's syllabus, so this means they will test up to level 5 verbs where the learning outcome permits this.

CIMA will limit the number of lower level questions in the exam – so that students will not be able to achieve the pass mark solely based on correctly answering knowledge and comprehension questions. Higher level questions, requiring candidates to demonstrate application, analysis and evaluation skills must be answered correctly for the pass mark to be reached.

Passing the E3 Objective Test exam

Tackling Objective Test Questions (OTQs)

- Read, and **re-read the question** to ensure you fully understand what is being asked.

- When starting to read a question, especially one with a lengthy scenario, **read the requirement first**. You will then find yourself considering the requirement as you read the data in the scenario, helping you to focus on exactly what you have to do.

- **Do not spend too much time on one question** - remember you should spend 1½ minutes, on average, per question.

- If you cannot decide between two answers – look carefully and decide whether for one of the options you are making an unnecessary assumption – **do not be afraid of trusting your gut instinct**.

- **Do not keep changing your mind** – research has shown that the 1st answer that appeals to you is often the correct one.

- Remember that marks are awarded for correct answers, and marks will not be deducted for incorrect answers. Therefore **answer every single question**, even ones you are unsure of.

- Always submit an answer for a given question even if you do not know the answer - **never leave any answers blank**.

- **Pace yourself** - you will need to work through the exam at the right speed. Too fast and your accuracy may suffer, too slow and you may run out of time. Use this Kit to practice your time keeping and approach to answering each question.

- If you are unsure about anything, remember to **ask the test administrator** before the test begins. Once the clock begins ticking, interruptions will not be allowed.

- Remember to **keep moving on!** You may be presented with a question which you simply cannot answer due to difficulty or if the wording is too vague. If you have only approximately 90 seconds per question, and you find yourself spending five minutes determining the answer for a question then your time management skills are poor and you are wasting valuable time.

- If you finish the exam with time to spare, use the rest of the time to **review your answers** and to make sure that you answered every OTQ.

Demonstrating your understanding of E3

The E3 examiner will expect you to demonstrate the following:

Strategic perspective	You must be able to **identify, analyse** and **evaluate** the ways an entity can organise its resources to meet stakeholder expectations and to achieve competitive advantage in the context of its external environment.
Making reasonable recommendations and strategic choices	The strategies you recommend, or the advice you give to management, must be **appropriate** for the organisation: it must be **suitable** to the organisation's strategic position; **acceptable** to its key stakeholders; and **feasible** given the organisation's resources and capabilities.
Importance of information systems	You must be able to **evaluate** how well an organisation's information system are supporting its business strategies and how information technology or information system could contribute to successful strategy implementation.
Leadership and change management	You need to be able to **evaluate** the tools and techniques which can be used to successfully implement a change programme, and to **recommend** appropriate leadership styles in different organisational change contexts.
Carry out appropriate calculations and interpret the results of them	An organisation needs to **measure** its performance in order to assess how successful its strategies have been. You must be able to perform appropriate calculations and also to **interpret**, or **analyse**, the results of those calculations.
Strategic awareness	Remember this is a Strategic level paper, and you will be expected to demonstrate the skills and abilities of a strategic **leader**; developing and implementing strategies which ensure long-term, **sustainable success** for organisations.

All OTQs in all the exams are worth the same number of marks, both in this Kit and in the real exam. However this is an approximate guide: some OTQs are very short and just require a factual selection, which you either know or you don't, while others are more complex, which will inevitably take more time. Note that the real exam will be balanced such that the 'difficulty' of the exam will be fair for all students – the OTQs in this Kit have also been balanced in a similar way.

Using the solutions and feedback

Avoid looking at the answer until you have finished a question. It can be very tempting to do so, but unless you give the question a proper attempt under exam conditions you will not know how you would have coped with it in the real exam scenario.

When you do look at the answer, compare it with your own and give some thought to why your answer was different, if it was.

If you did not reach the correct answer make sure that you work through the explanation or workings provided, to see where you went wrong. If you think that you do not understand the principle involved, work through and revise the point again, to ensure that you will understand it if it occurs in the exam.

Objective Test questions

1 Fundamentals of strategic management

1.1 BPP began life as a training company. Lecturers had to prepare course material. This was offered for sale in a bookshop in the BPP building.

Owing to unanticipated demand, BPP began offering its material to other colleges, in the UK and world-wide.

BPP Learning Media, which began as a small offshoot of BPPs training activities, is now a leading publisher in the market for targeted study material for the examinations of several professional bodies.

This is an example of which approach to strategy?

☐ Rational
☐ Emergent
☐ Incremental
☐ Planned

1.2 Which of the following are criticisms of the rational strategic model?

☐ It focuses attention on the objectives of an organisation
☐ It focuses on the long term even if the market is extremely dynamic
☐ It focuses on resources rather than environmental factors
☐ Generating strategy is a cultural and psychological process that cannot be forced
☐ It only allows ideas that have been generated through the formal process

1.3 What is corporate governance?

☐ Legal rules governing the behaviour of directors
☐ The system by which organisations are directed and controlled
☐ The system by which stock markets control the behaviour of public companies
☐ The system which organisations use to direct and control the behaviour of senior management

1.4 According to the rational planning model, in which order should the activities listed as 1 - 5 below be carried out?

1   Environmental analysis
2   Objectives
3   Mission
3   Position audit
5   Corporate appraisal

☐ (3), (2), (4), (5), (1)
☐ (3), (2), (1), (5), (4)
☐ (2), (3), (1), (4), (5)
☐ (3), (2), (1), (4), (5)

1.5 Sometimes strategy can come about as a largely unintended result of the everyday activities, decisions and processes that take place at all levels within an organisation.

What is this type of strategy called?

☐ Rational strategy
☐ Strategic drift
☐ Emergent strategy
☐ Unrealised strategy

BPP
LEARNING MEDIA

1.6 Indicate whether the following approaches to strategic planning are formal or informal.

Opportunistic	Informal ☐	Formal ☐
Incremental	Informal ☐	Formal ☐
Rational model	Informal ☐	Formal ☐

1.7 Bone Group, which manufactures valves and pumps, and provides engineering services, has recruited three top executives from the automotive industry, as part of its long term intention to bring lean manufacturing methods to the firm from the car industry.

Which one of the following best describes Bone Group's decision to introduce lean manufacturing methods?

☐ A corporate strategy and a deliberate strategy
☐ An operational strategy and a deliberate strategy
☐ A business unit strategy and a deliberate strategy
☐ A business unit strategy and an emergent strategy

1.8 Governance is an issue for which bodies corporate?

☐ Not-for-profit bodies only
☐ All commercial and not-for-profit bodies
☐ Listed companies only
☐ Limited companies only

1.9 Which of the following is NOT a feature of poor corporate governance?

☐ Boards composed of relatively elderly directors
☐ Lack of supervision
☐ Lack of involvement of board
☐ Domination by a single individual

1.10 Strategic direction has been described in terms of resource based approach and environmental fit.

What of the following is an advantage of a resource based approach?

☐ Ensures products are generated following extensive market research
☐ Exploits the organisation's distinctive competences
☐ Exploits the distinctive competences of competitors
☐ Allows the organisation to exploit opportunities

2 Corporate objectives and stakeholders

2.1 PPR operates gyms in many cities of the world. Before the advent of social media, PPR tended to ignore the complaints of individual clients. Today, PPR's management is aware that social media provides a way for individual clients to record and publish positive and negative comments about their experiences at a PPR gym.

Which of the following statements best describes the impact of social media on the stakeholder categorisation of PPR's individual customers?

☐ Customers have moved from key players to keep informed.
☐ Customers have shifted from keep satisfied to key players.
☐ Customers have shifted from minimal effort to keep informed.
☐ Customers have shifted from minimal effort to keep satisfied.

2.2 PQ plc is a furniture retailing firm. At a recent presentation to investment analysts and financial journalists, PQ's FD gave a very optimistic forecast for the firm's future, suggesting that revenue would treble over the next three years and profits and dividends would increase by 80%. The FD prepared his forecast in a hurry and had not had it confirmed by anybody else within PQ.

The FD also did not mention in his presentation that PQ's home government was considering taking legal action against PQ for underpayment of excise duties and had made a claim for large damages. If this claim was to be successful it would materially affect PQ's profit.

The situation above contains a potential conflict with the fundamental ethical principle of:

☐ Objectivity
☐ Integrity
☐ Confidentiality
☐ Professional Competence
☐ Professional Behaviour

2.3 KPN is a publicly quoted company which manufactures and distributes alcoholic drinks.

Which of the following arguments best justify its sustainability plans as being in the interest of investors?

Select all that apply.

☐ Sustainability can help KPN reduce costs and improve efficiency.
☐ Sustainability can help reduce the environmental impact of KPN.
☐ Sustainability can help KPN lead the way in shaping society.
☐ Sustainability can help KPN to comply with laws and regulations and to avoid fines.
☐ Sustainability can help protect KPN's reputation with stakeholders.

2.4 Stakeholder mapping looks at stakeholders and their impact on strategy.

Which TWO of the following elements are assessed in this theory?

☐ Level of diversity in the portfolio
☐ Level of interest
☐ Level of financial investment
☐ Level of control
☐ Level of competition
☐ Level of power

2.5 Mito Care is a not for profit eye hospital and research centre.

Which one of the following statements is likely to relate to Mito Care's vision, rather than its mission statement?

☐ Mito Care offers the highest level of patient care throughout country X.
☐ Mito Care consultants strive to continually improve surgical techniques.
☐ Mito Care will be the global leader in cutting edge eye surgery.
☐ Mito Care will continue to transform patient care through its continuing research focus.
☐ Mito Care places patient care before all else.

BPP
LEARNING MEDIA

2.6 JLR is a utilities provider that is based in a country that has very tough laws against businesses trying to win orders through bribing domestic and foreign government officials and politicians. JLR wishes to be invited to submit a tender for contracts in Country E, a developing country with an unelected government.

Which of the following is the best way for JLR to ensure it is invited to tender for the work in Country E?

- ☐ Appoint a government minister from Country E as a Non-Executive Director of JLR
- ☐ Stress to the government of JLR's home country the jobs that winning the contract could create and lobby them to ask the government of Country E to include JLR in the tender
- ☐ Undertake a promotional campaign amongst the population of Country E that stresses the good CSR record of JLR
- ☐ Fund a programme of inoculations for the children of Country E to protect them from a widespread and fatal disease

---

2.7 CIMA's research has identified ten elements which are needed to successfully embed sustainability within an organisation's culture. These elements are grouped under three headings: strategy and oversight; execution and alignment; and performance and reporting.

Identify which of these three headings the elements listed below relate to:

Understanding of the key sustainability drivers of an organisation	☐ Strategy and oversight	☐ Execution and alignment	☐ Performance and reporting
Extensive and effective sustainability training	☐ Strategy and oversight	☐ Execution and alignment	☐ Performance and reporting
Integration of the key sustainability drivers into the organisation's strategy	☐ Strategy and oversight	☐ Execution and alignment	☐ Performance and reporting
Champions to promote sustainability and celebrate success	☐ Strategy and oversight	☐ Execution and alignment	☐ Performance and reporting

---

2.8 CIMA's Code of Ethics identifies five categories of threat which could compromise an accountant's ability to comply with the fundamental ethical principles.

Which one of these threats occurs if an accountant is promoting a client's position to the extent that the accountant's subsequent objectivity is compromised?

- ☐ Self interest threat
- ☐ Self review threat
- ☐ Advocacy threat
- ☐ Intimidation threat

2.9 Large companies often include a reference to social responsibility in their mission statements.

Which of the aspirations below reflect a genuine concern for socially responsible behaviour?

Select all that apply.

- ☐ To provide good working conditions and decent rewards for all employees
- ☐ To conform with legislation in reducing the harmful waste products from our processes to an acceptable level
- ☐ To keep employees informed of policy, progress and problems
- ☐ To pay at least the minimum wage to all employees
- ☐ To support the local community and preserve the environment

2.10 A CIMA member was asked to identify a situation in which he was exposed to an ethical dilemma relating to compliance with a fundamental ethical principle, and to explain what steps were taken to resolve the ethical conflict, to which he responded:

'I had heard rumours that one of our suppliers was employing child labour. I followed internal procedures to determine the appropriate course of action, which resulted in me notifying my immediate manager. My manager assured me that the situation posed no significant threat to our business or its reputation, so there was no need to investigate it any further, or seek any external advice.'

Which of the following describes the accountant's actions?

- ☐ EXCELLENT: He identified the facts, ethical issues and ethical principles; he notified the appropriate persons and resolved the issue.
- ☐ GOOD: He identified the facts, notified and consulted the appropriate persons and resolved the issue.
- ☐ POOR: He failed to identify the facts, ethical issues or ethical principles. However the appropriate persons were notified and the issue was resolved.
- ☐ VERY POOR: He failed to identify the facts. No professional advice was sought and the issue remained unresolved.

2.11 For a number of years, companies in the south west of Country X have complained that the poor infrastructure and communication links in the region are damaging their competitiveness.

The government of County X wants to attract foreign investment into the country, and is proposing to create a new economic zone in the south west of the country. There has been significant resistance to the plans by local companies, but in response to this the government has promised to improve the infrastructure in the region and to introduce super-fast broadband.

Which one of the following best describes the conflict resolution strategy the government appears to be using?

- ☐ Exercise of power
- ☐ Satisficing
- ☐ Sequential attention
- ☐ Side payments

2.12 N Co manufactures and sells chocolate and other confectionery. N obtains much of its cocoa from suppliers in Country Y, a relatively poor country. N has recently announced that 1% of its profits each year will be spent on community projects in Y.

According to Caroll & Buchholtz's classifications of corporate social responsibility, which kind of responsibility does N Co's proposal relate to?

☐   Economic responsibility
☐   Ethical responsibility
☐   Philanthropic responsibility
☐   Legal responsibility

2.13 The directors at T Co have been debating the extent to which they need to consider the interests of different stakeholder groups when determining the company's strategy.

The CEO believes that T should only be concerned with the short-term interests of its shareholders, and so it should focus on the strategic options which help it to make the greatest profits in the short term.

However, the marketing director has argued that T should take a longer-term view. He is concerned that the CEO's approach could be detrimental to T's corporate image, and could affect its ability to deliver value to its shareholders in the longer term.

Which of Johnson, Scholes and Whittington's ethical stances are the two directors adopting?

CEO:

☐   Enlightened self-interest
☐   Laissez-faire
☐   Multiple stakeholder obligations
☐   Shaper of society

Marketing director:

☐   Enlightened self-interest
☐   Laissez-faire
☐   Multiple stakeholder obligations
☐   Shaper of society

2.14 Braithwaite and Drahos highlight that, when analysing an organisation's stakeholders, it is important to consider 'civil society' groups and organisations.

Which THREE of the following are best described as part of 'civil society'?

☐   Governments and regulatory bodies
☐   Trades unions
☐   Local residents concerned about the construction of a new factory
☐   Non-governmental organisations
☐   Environmental groups

3 The environment and uncertainty

3.1 CC sells garden machinery in a mature market. It is suffering falling sales volumes and profits. Prices and costs in the market have not changed.

Which of the following are the most likely causes of this?

Select all that apply.

- ☐ Increased competitive rivalry
- ☐ Market entry by new competitors
- ☐ Increased supplier power
- ☐ Increased buyer power
- ☐ Increased threat from substitutes

3.2 GPS is a failing retailer of children's clothing. You are part of the team that has been called in by investors to turn GPS around. Your priorities are to restore it to profitability quickly and then, later, to decide a long-term business strategy.

Which of the following correctly describes the sequence in which the team should use different types of analysis, initially to improve the short-term profitability of GPS, and then determine its longer-term strategic direction?

- ☐ PEST analysis, Competitor analysis, Industry life cycle analysis, Porter's five forces analysis
- ☐ Competitor analysis, Porter's five forces analysis, Industry life cycle analysis, PEST analysis
- ☐ Porter's five forces analysis, PEST analysis, Competitor analysis, Industry life cycle analysis
- ☐ Industry life cycle analysis, PEST analysis, Porter's five forces analysis, Competitor analysis

3.3 STI designs and manufactures smartphones. It is considering using foresight techniques in its strategic formulation activities. These techniques include scenario planning, morphological analysis, and visioning.

Identify THREE major benefits of foresight techniques to STI from the list below:

- ☐ They improve management's communication and awareness of complex issues affecting STI.
- ☐ They provide management with clarity on the future of the smartphone industry.
- ☐ They provide some consensus amongst management on what STI should research in future.
- ☐ They will enable STI's management to calculate the forecast earnings from new projects.
- ☐ They help STI's management to concentrate on the longer term despite the high uncertainty.

3.4 Pony has recently launched a new version of its acclaimed and very popular games console. In response to the widespread adoption of ultra-fast broadband, and despite concerns regarding piracy, the console has been designed to allow players to download the games they want to play rather than requiring a physical optical disc to be inserted in the console. The console has been labelled as a 'must have for any gamer' by most of the industry publications.

In the initial launch phase of the console which of the following statements is most likely to be true?

- ☐ Prices will be low and demand will be very high.
- ☐ Prices will be high to match high demand.
- ☐ Prices will be high and demand will be relatively low.
- ☐ Prices will be low to stimulate initial product demand.

3.5 AAA is considering whether to invest in a project. The initial NPV calculation is negative. However, before the project is rejected the Finance Director believes the company should consider other factors.

Which of the following relate to real options?

Select all that apply.

☐ Follow on investments should be factored into the initial investment decision.
☐ AAA should consider whether the project can be subdivided.
☐ Better information may become available to AAA if it delays its decision.
☐ AAA should establish whether it is able to abandon the project part way through.
☐ The discount factor may be adjusted for risk.

3.6 B is a European Bank, providing a range of banking products to individual customers. It operates through a network of branches and, five years ago, it invested €600 million to open branches in Z Land. At the time, Z Land had a rapidly growing economy, and B considered there were good retail banking opportunities in Z Land. NW Bank, which is the major state-owned bank in Z Land accounts for half of the retail banking business in the country and so holds a position of market dominance. There are also some well-established foreign banks that hold 35% of the market between them. The rest of the market in Z Land is held by small regional banks.

Traditionally, there has been little customer loyalty in the banking industry in Z Land. The majority of bank customers are individuals who can choose to bank with any of the local or foreign banks operating in the country. Z Land permits the free movement of funds, so NW Bank has access to cash both inside and outside of Z Land. Z Land's government encourages foreign investment. However, the government is also very supportive of NW Bank.

Identify whether the following competitive forces in relation to the banking industry in Z Land are strong, weak or neutral?

Competitive rivalry	☐ Strong	☐ Weak	☐ Neutral
Bargaining power of customers	☐ Strong	☐ Weak	☐ Neutral
Threat of new entrants	☐ Strong	☐ Weak	☐ Neutral

3.7 DD is a small charity with a relatively low profile, which helps elderly people access a range of services via the internet. DD employs 25 skilled workers in a variety of roles, but relies upon the help of a further 40 volunteers.

The recent recession has had a negative impact on DD's fundraising, as both donations and government grants have fallen. This has caused DD to cut back on the range of services it offers. The trustees are now concerned about the long-term impact that this rationalisation will have on DD's reputation. To make matters worse, some of DD's staff have left for other charities, having been lured by better job security.

Keen to bolster the charity sector in DD's country, the government has announced a relaxation in the rules on charities working together, and with private companies. As a result DD has been approached by EE, a larger and better funded charity. EE offers complementary services to those offered by DD such as helping teenagers access government career services.

Which of the following factors would be considered as THREATS to DD:

Select all that apply.

☐ DD has a low profile in the charity sector
☐ Reduced scope of activities
☐ The economic recession, leading to reduced funding
☐ Loss of staff to more secure charities
☐ Merger with EE

3.8   Magic Moments is a travel agency based in Europe, focusing on the exclusive end of the cruise market, and serving destinations outside the Eurozone.

Which THREE of the following would have a serious direct negative impact on sales of Magic Moments' holidays?

- ☐   Rise in interest rates
- ☐   Advances in airline technology
- ☐   Devaluation of the euro
- ☐   Increasing popularity of activity holidays
- ☐   Rise in the market wage rate for ship croupiers
- ☐   Increase in safety legislation regarding cruise ships

3.9   Where high levels of uncertainty exist, an organisation may employ scenario planning, allowing it to model environmental outcomes based on changing assumptions.

Place the numbers 1-5 against the following key stages in scenario planning to indicate the correct sequence in which they should be undertaken (with '1' being the earliest and '5' being the last).

Defining the scope of the project, and identifying major stakeholders	☐
Developing quantitative models used to formulate competitive strategies	☐
Developing learning scenarios and identifying further research needs	☐
Identifying key trends and areas of uncertainty	☐
Constructing initial scenarios and checking them for consistency	☐

3.10   **Which of the following would be classified as forecasting techniques suitable for use by an organisation within an uncertain environment?**

Select all that apply.

- ☐   Visioning
- ☐   Foresight
- ☐   Time series
- ☐   Regression
- ☐   Delphi method

4 Resources and capabilities

4.1   XPO sells, installs and maintains office photocopiers. It has noticed that more of its clients are complaining of more frequent breakdowns in their systems which, due to a shortage of skilled engineers, are taking a long time to repair. Investigations have revealed that the cause of this problem is that customers have been sold systems that are too small for their requirements.

Which activities in Porter's Value Chain need to be improved at XPO?

Select all that apply.

- ☐   Operations
- ☐   Technology development
- ☐   Human resource management
- ☐   Service
- ☐   Marketing and sales

4.2 BB is an established manufacturer of sports watches, especially well regarded by runners and cyclists. It has taken the decision to incorporate Global Positioning System (GPS) in all of its products. Its immediate customer, a large sports equipment retailer, is not in favour of the change. However, amongst customers who have previously purchased BB products there have been strong expressions of support.

Which of the following statements best describes the situation outlined above?

- ☐ Value chain management
- ☐ Upstream supply chain management
- ☐ Downstream supply chain management
- ☐ Customer relationship management

4.3 FDJ is a frozen food range which has captured a 60% share of the market. Overall, market growth has fallen to 4% per year in the past five years and is forecast to fall further. The manufacturer of FDJ has used the Boston Consulting Group matrix to decide to reduce investment in the range.

Which of the following arguments justifies this decision?

- ☐ Mature products may not repay the opportunity cost of additional investment in them due to low margins and the danger of decline
- ☐ Products with small relative market shares may be uncompetitive due to their failure to benefit from economies of scale
- ☐ A low industry growth rate will increase the current cash flows available from a product
- ☐ A new product in a high growth market is risky and a firm cannot support a large number of them

4.4 Some of the cashiers at DEF Bank have become concerned about the length of the queues which have been forming as customers wait to be served. They have mentioned this to their managers, and the managers have suggested that DEF should try to gather information about the way other companies control the length of their queues to see if DEF can learn from this.

Currently, DEF has compared its performance with a supermarket, a railway station and an airport – all of which are regarded as having very efficient queuing processes.

What type of comparison is DEF undertaking?

- ☐ Internal benchmarking
- ☐ Competitive benchmarking
- ☐ Functional benchmarking
- ☐ Historical benchmarking

4.5 **A new product is being introduced by a small player into a growth market. How would the product be classified in the BCG matrix?**

- ☐ Question mark
- ☐ Star
- ☐ Dog
- ☐ Cash cow

4.6 **Which of the following are drivers of Shareholder Value Added (SVA)?**

Select all that apply.

- ☐ Effective rate of tax to sales ratio
- ☐ Company's cost of capital to sales ratio
- ☐ Operating profit to sales ratio
- ☐ Sector P/E ratio
- ☐ Dividend to net earnings ratio

4.7 The management of BPM believes that the firm is 'stuck in the middle' and wishes to use Porter's Value Chain to understand how to become an differentiator in its industry. It is devising a project plan to do this.

Identify the correct sequence in which BPM should undertake the following activities in the course of value chain analysis (with '1' being the activity which is undertaken first, and '5' being the activity which is undertaken last).

Identify how additional value can be generated by each activity performed ☐

Evaluate the requirements of BPM's customers ☐

Re-engineer activities where additional value can be added; consider reducing those
that do not add significant value ☐

Create a multi-disciplinary project team ☐

Identify which activities add value to customers and categorise them within the value chain ☐

4.8 **Which one of the following is NOT an aim of strategic supply chain management?**

☐ Reduce the number of suppliers
☐ Focus on customers of high potential value
☐ Closer relationships including linked systems
☐ Frequently changing suppliers

4.9 There have been criticisms of the product life cycle's usefulness as a forecasting tool.

Identify TWO reasons for this from the list below.

☐ The product is affected by environmental issues outside the control of the company.
☐ The product is affected by internal decisions about the level of resources given to the product.
☐ The product will have a finite life-span.
☐ The product's sales will move through distinct phases affecting sales and cash flows.

4.10 **Which of the following is NOT an example of outbound logistics as described in the value chain model?**

☐ Transporting
☐ Packaging
☐ Warehousing
☐ Selling

5 Developing and evaluating strategic options

5.1 DD is a highly successful clothes retailer operating in its home country F, which is in Europe. DD is the market leader in its home country but in the last three years its market share has fallen due to increased price competition from its two nearest rivals in country F. As a result, in the last six months DD has expanded its operations into two other European countries through the acquisition of an established small chain of clothes retailers, based in one of those countries.

Which form of international expansion strategy has DD undertaken through the acquisition of the small chain of supermarkets in the two other European countries?

☐ A franchising strategy
☐ A transnational strategy
☐ An exporting strategy
☐ A foreign direct investment strategy

5.2 QS manufactures a wide range of sports clothing for a wide variety of customer groups. QS has been advised that it is 'stuck in the middle' according to Porter's Generic Strategy model. Management has decided to adopt a cost focus strategy and become a cost leader in just a simple narrow segment of the broader industry it already serves.

Identify the statements below that are true in relation to this decision:

Select all that apply.

☐ QS will gain barriers to entry in its niche segment
☐ QS will benefit from economies of scale by increasing its total output of clothing
☐ QS will gain higher profits from an exclusive position and higher prices
☐ QS will need to reduce its product range
☐ QS will be more exposed to risk from a decline in this segment

(5.3) **Which of the following statements is/are true?**

1. As businesses move towards being global organisations, thought needs to be given to changes in their organisation structure.

2. When starting to operate in a new country, a company should work through a joint venture rather than via an agent.

☐ Both (1) and (2)
☐ (1) only
☐ (2) only
☐ Neither (1) or (2)

5.4 Beta plc is set to launch a new high-technology product. Demand is forecast to be very strong due to a combination of the product's capability and critically acclaimed design. R&D costs have been very high and Beta plc is keen to recoup these are quickly as possible.

Which one of the following pricing strategies would be used to meet the objective of repaying R&D costs as quickly as possible?

☐ Price skimming
☐ Price penetration
☐ Cost plus pricing
☐ Discount pricing

(5.5) **Which of the following are possible disadvantages of a joint venture arrangement?**

(i) Disagreements between the venture partners over management and marketing strategy
(ii) Profits have to be shared among the venture partners
(iii) Confidential information about the partners could get shared between them

☐ (i) & (ii) only
☐ (i) & (iii) only
☐ (ii) & (iii) only
☐ (i), (ii) & (iii)

5.6 SNER is an energy producing company that at present only operates coal-fired power stations. A Chartered Global Management Accountant (CGMA) working for SNER was asked to evaluate whether SNER should invest in a business to generate electricity by wind and solar power stations.

The CGMA wrote the following response:

'According to Ansoff's matrix, this would be an example of market development by our company. Using the Suitability, Acceptability, Feasibility (SAF) framework of Johnson, Scholes and Whittington the investment is Suitable because we have all the core competences needed for generating electricity by wind and solar power technologies. It will be Acceptable to investors because they have shown a willingness to invest in energy generation and are accustomed to risk and long payback investments. It will be Feasible because regulatory authorities will recognise that SNER has a good safety record.'

Which of the following best describes the response from the CGMA?

☐ EXCELLENT: A correct evaluation has been provided based on a sound understanding of Ansoff's matrix and SAF analysis, and it has applied both correctly.

☐ GOOD: Appropriate evaluation using SAF and core competences but contains some misundertanding about Ansoff's matrix.

☐ POOR: Evaluation is based on a flawed assessment of core competences and incorrect applications of Ansoff's matrix and SAF analysis.

☐ UNACCEPTABLE: The CGMA has shown no understanding of core competences, nor of the application of Ansoff's matrix and SAF analysis.

5.7 Claire Ltd is considering a project with the following revenue stream:

Year	Investment $000	Variable costs $000	Sales $000	Net cash flows $000
0	(10,000)			
1		(4,000)	9,000	5,000
2		(4,000)	9,000	5,000
3		(4,000)	9,000	5,000

The company's cost of capital is 5%.

Assuming the project has a three year life-span, by what percentage will total sales over the life of the project have to fall for the project to produce a zero net present value?

☐ 14.8%
☐ 26.6%
☐ 33.2%
☐ 36.2%

5.8 **Which of the following is unlikely to be a consequence of an organisation's pursuit of a strategy of globalisation?**

☐ Increased exposure to political risk
☐ Greater costs associated with natural disasters
☐ Increased merger and acquisition activity
☐ Taller vertical organisation structures

(5.9) Indicate which of the following are benefits of Lynch's Expansion Matrix and which are drawbacks of it.

Can generate multiple strategic options	☐ Benefit	☐ Drawback
Requires interpretation to make it fit the circumstances of the organisation	☐ Benefit	☐ Drawback
Not sufficient on its own to determine strategy	☐ Benefit	☐ Drawback
Simple visual presentation of complex ideas	☐ Benefit	☐ Drawback
Does not include means of achieving growth	☐ Benefit	☐ Drawback
Long established and familiar to management	☐ Benefit	☐ Drawback

5.10 UNS manufactures women's uniforms under contract from the armed forces in its home country. It has several competitors and it receives no more than 20% of the total orders for women's clothes from the armed forces.

UNS is considering four strategic options, shown below.

Classify each of the strategic options as to whether it is an example of market penetration; market development; product development; or diversification.

Purchase another woman's uniform manufacturer whose sole business is supplying the armed forces in UNS's home country	
Purchase a men's uniform manufacturer, based in another country, whose sole business is supplying the armed forces in UNS's home country	
Tender for that contracts to supply women's uniforms to the armed forces of another country	
Purchase a men's uniform manufacturer, based in another country, that has contracts with the armed forces of several countries	

6 Creating an IT strategy

6.1 X operates a commercial lettings agency. A lettings agent arranges the rental and management of commercial buildings such as offices, factories and warehouses.

X has a website on which it advertises all of its properties, and which allows customers to view the property details, such as internal photographs and floor layout. X's website also uses a range of interactive technologies including geographical location and map facilities, links to external information sites to show other businesses located close to properties, and links to local government websites.

Which one of the following best describes the range of interactive technologies used by X within its website?

☐   Competence syndication
☐   Mash-up
☐   Information sharing
☐   Social media

6.2 DTI is an airline operator that provides budget air travel. Passengers are required to book through its website. It has recently redesigned its website to take advantage of Web 2.0 innovations.

DTI's website enables the customer to check the schedules of the flights, and to book online. Customers are also able to manage their check-in and print off essential documentation to enable them to board the aircraft. The website contains pages that show weather forecasts and local news for each destination, drawn from electronic feeds from the news websites of outside organisations. Customers are encouraged to upload photographs from recent trips with DTI and to write descriptions and allocate grades for the destinations they visited. During the booking process, additional pages appear that enable the customer to book transport or accommodation at the destination from third party suppliers.

Which of the following uses of Web 2.0 applications is missing from the website of DTI?

☐ Social media
☐ Mash-ups
☐ Viral advertising
☐ Competence syndication

6.3 Which of the following terms relates specifically to the selection of software and hardware within an organisation?

☐ Information systems (IS) strategy
☐ Information management (IM) strategy
☐ Information technology (IT) strategy
☐ Business strategy

6.4 A very useful approach for a business to decide what information its Management Information System (MIS) must report on is to specify the business's critical success factors (CSF). Performance indicators are then specified for each CSF, and the MIS must be able to report in terms of these indicators.

Which of the following would be appropriate measures for assessing how well a retailing organisation is achieving its CSF of offering excellent customer service?

Select all that apply.

☐ Queue lengths at tills
☐ Number of customer complaints
☐ Number of returns
☐ Customer satisfaction scores
☐ Employee satisfaction scores

6.5 Of the following, which TWO sources of information are most likely to be used in a decision support system (DSS)?

☐ Information with a long time frame.
☐ External and internal information.
☐ Information with a short time frame.
☐ Detailed information.
☐ Both qualitative and quantitative information.

6.6 Catseye is a producer of frozen foods that sells its products to major retail chains in many countries around the world.

Following the failure of its expensive investment in new information technology, the board of Catseye was advised by consultants to replace its former Manager of Computer Services with an Information Technology Director at Board level.

Select the reasons below that best justify making information strategy a senior management role at Catseye rather than something that should be left to technical experts within the IT department.

Select all that apply.

☐ It is a potential source of competitive advantage for Catseye that should be managed strategically as well as operationally.

☐ Creation of a senior role for information will help Catseye attract and retain better staff due to the higher pay and better careers available with Catseye.

☐ Changes in information strategy can have significant impacts on internal and external stakeholders that need to be handled strategically.

☐ A senior role avoids duplication of expenditure, systems, and data in the divisions of Catseye and improves integration.

☐ Expenditure on information systems is significant and often requires evaluation against both strategic initiatives and business operations.

6.7 Which of the following activities will fall within the information management (IM) strategy?

Select all that apply.

☐ Planning and controlling IS developments.
☐ Reviewing the communications infrastructure.
☐ Allocating human resources within the IT department.
☐ Assessing the information needs of the business.
☐ Reviewing the latest technological developments for ways to exploit them.

6.8 **If an organisation has a robust information management (IM) strategy in place, which one of the following is most likely to be evident at the organisation?**

☐ Clear prioritisation of development projects and efficient use of the resources available.
☐ Minimum standards for software and hardware.
☐ Technological innovations being used to gain competitive advantage.
☐ IT developments reflecting the needs of the business.

6.9 **The creation of an IS strategy can be justified on many grounds: which of the following are NOT relevant or correct justifications?**

Select all the apply.

☐ Business spends a lot of money on IS and IT.
☐ An IS strategy is critical to the success of many organisations.
☐ IS and IT can be used for competitive advantage.
☐ IS and IT affect some levels of management.
☐ IS and IT affect the way management information is created and presented.
☐ IS and IT may need effective management to obtain maximum benefit from them.
☐ Information systems involve many stakeholders inside and outside the organisation.

6.10 Which one of the following statements about expert systems is NOT correct?

☐ An expert system must be designed from scratch.

☐ An expert system requires no human input before a decision is taken.

☐ The rules of an expert system are derived by experimentation and learning.

☐ The rules governing an expert system can be updated.

6.11 LDI and WTS are both supermarkets, but LDI pursues a low price strategy, while WTS follows a differentiation strategy based on the high quality of the products it sells.

You have recently been comparing the performance measurement systems in LDI and WTS and noticed that both supermarkets identified 'having the right product mix available on the shelves for customers to buy' as one of their critical success factors (CSFs).

According to Rockart's model, which of the following best describes the source of the CSF?

☐ The company and its situation in the industry

☐ The external environment

☐ The industry that the company is in

☐ Temporal factors

7 Using IT strategically

7.1 BBL is a small private training company. Up to now, all of its training has been carried out in the classroom. Recent market research carried out by BBL has indicated that there is an extensive market in online training, and the senior management team is considering moving into this area of business. Many of BBL's competitors are already offering online training facilities. BBL currently operates a website through which its classroom-based delegates can book onto courses, communicate via email with tutors, download course literature, and make payments for courses. Developing online training facilities would mean that BBL would need to develop facilities for online delivery of courses and it would also need to use other means of advertising its courses to a wider online audience.

Select forms of Web 2.0 applications which BBL should use to enable it to deliver and advertise its online tuition.

Select all that apply.

☐ CRM

☐ Webcasts

☐ Presentation software such as Microsoft Powerpoint

☐ Social media

7.2 The senior management team at KDN wishes to develop a performance management system to implement its new strategic direction.

Indicate the order in which KDN's management should undertake the following steps when developing their performance management system (with '1' being the earliest and '5' being the latest.)

Identify the Critical Success Factors of the strategy	
Set the targets for the organisations and its managers	
Set the strategic objectives of the organisation	
Establish mission of the organisation	
Establish the Key Performance Indicators	

BPP LEARNING MEDIA

7.3 The senior managers at SRB have been reviewing the progress the company has made in implementing its e-business strategy. They have noted that the company's website allows customers to place orders for SRB products and pay for them online, and the website also provides answers to frequently asked questions (FAQs). However, the website does not allow customers to create personalised accounts and does not capture information about customers' purchasing history which SRB's marketing department could use to target its marketing activities more precisely.

Which of the following stages in the introduction of e-business has SRB currently reached?

☐ Basic e-commerce
☐ E-business
☐ Integrated e-commerce
☐ Web presence

7.4 For some organisations, the way in which they manage information, and the quality of their information systems is a source of competitive advantage.

Which one of these examples does NOT confer competitive advantage?

☐ The introduction of an expert system to improve the decision making at a credit reference agency.

☐ Developing an Executive Information System that is more advanced than the competition.

☐ Being the first organisation to integrate the supply chain through the use of Electronic Data Interchange.

☐ Upgrading the nominal ledger to the most recent version of the package.

7.5 Which of the following is one of main advantages of an information system built around a database?

☐ The development of separate data sources
☐ Unlimited access and open communication
☐ End users exercise control over data
☐ Data integrity and the elimination of duplication

7.6 Lastsecond.com operates a web-based business offering reduced rate hotel rooms, satisfying the needs of hotel operators to boost utilisation and customers to find cheap holiday accommodation. Whilst the company is profitable its owners have expressed a desire to drive more value from the data it captures from its website. They plan to use a knowledge management programme to do this.

Indicate which knowledge management requirement each of the organisational tools of knowledge management (A – E below) best supports.

A   Creation of sharing culture
B   Database structure
C   Staff development and training
D   Intranet and extranet
E   Technological infrastructure

Creation of knowledge   ☐

Capture of knowledge   ☐

Storage of knowledge   ☐

Availability (dissemination) of knowledge   ☐

Utilisation of knowledge   ☐

7.7 **Which of the following statements are NOT true?**

Select all that apply.

☐ Big data is the storing of organisational data in digital form.

☐ Big data allows an increasing understanding and segmentation of customers.

☐ Big data is the creation and analysis of a large internal data warehouse used to store all of an organisation's data relating to customers, staff, operations and products.

☐ Big data can be used to improve the development of the next generation of products and services for organisations.

7.8 If an organisation is outsourcing some of its IT services, it is vital that the organisation knows what it can expect to receive from the outsource partner. However, it is equally important that the outsource partner also knows what the organisation expects from it.

Which one of the following documents is a contract which can be used to manage these expectations between an organisation and its outsource partners?

☐ The service level agreement
☐ The software supply agreement
☐ The operations agreement
☐ The project management agreement

7.9 **The main distinguishing feature of Web 2.0 applications (compared to earlier web applications) is:**

☐ Improved graphics
☐ E-commerce capability
☐ Broadband connectivity
☐ Increased user participation

7.10 **Identify whether the following statements about information networks are true or false.**

Only employees are able to access information on an extranet.   ☐ True   ☐ False

Intronets allow suppliers and customers to gain privileged access to data held by the host.   ☐ True   ☐ False

---

7.11 One of the characteristics which Peter Senge identified as being crucial to learning organisations is that of 'team learning'.

Which one of the following best describes team learning?

☐ The recognition that organisations learn only through individuals who learn

☐ The assumptions and generalisations which influence how people understand the world and how they take action

☐ The process of aligning and developing the capacities of a team to create the results its members truly desire

☐ The capacity to hold a shared picture of the future that a team or organisation seeks to create

8 Strategic marketing

8.1   Chimmy Shoo is an exclusive and expensive manufacturer of ladies' fashion shoes. The company employs its own design team, and makes the majority of its shoes to order in its own workshop in Milan, Italy. To place an order the customer must visit the single shop that the company operates, to have their precise foot measurements taken. Chimmy Shoo's customers tend to be very wealthy individuals with large amounts of disposable income. Although the majority live in and around Northern Italy, a significant number of customers visit Milan annually to purchase one or more pairs of custom-made shoes.

Chimmy Shoo's customers are given personal accounts and are invoiced at the end of each month. The founder of the company is keen to invest in new technologies, but is aware that the company has a limited IT budget and wishes to spend this wisely.

Select the most suitable of the following investments for Chimmy Shoo:

- ☐   Automated warehousing
- ☐   In-store self-service check-outs
- ☐   Computer-aided design
- ☐   e-Procurement

8.2   When considering a tangible product the marketing mix consists of four Ps. When a service is being considered, three additional Ps are added to give a marketing mix of seven Ps.

Which of the following are the additional Ps which are added to the traditional marketing mix to form the service marketing mix?

Select all that apply.

- ☐   People
- ☐   Processes
- ☐   Physical evidence
- ☐   Promotion
- ☐   Place

8.3   **Which of the following sources of information would be the most suitable to use to monitor market trends?**

Select all that apply.

- ☐   The internal company sales database.
- ☐   Information received from market research agencies on sector sales.
- ☐   Government forecasts of population demographics.
- ☐   Competitor sales activity analysis.
- ☐   Customer satisfaction surveys.

8.4   **Identify whether the following statements about marketing and the internet are true or false:**

The internet promotes transparent pricing

- ☐   True
- ☐   False

E-marketing is primarily useful for customer retention rather than customer acquisition

- ☐   True
- ☐   False

8.5 The internet and on-line marketing techniques can play a very important role in relationship marketing, particularly customer acquisition.

However, which one of the following is most useful for customer extension rather than customer acquisition?

☐ Search engines
☐ Comparison sites
☐ Recommendations
☐ Affiliate marketing

8.6 Marketing planning is subordinate to corporate planning but makes a significant contribution to it and is concerned with many of the same issues.

Which of the following is a contribution that can best be made by marketing to the overall strategic plan?

☐ It ensures the profit gap is filled
☐ It sets production levels
☐ It ensures that the company is pursuing effective policies to promote its products and services
☐ It controls marketing assistants' salaries

8.7 **Which of the following are features of customer relationship marketing?**

(i) It devotes marketing resources to maintaining and exploiting an organisation's existing customer base
(ii) It focuses on establishing loyalty among customers
(iii) It tries to have only low to moderate contact with customers

☐ (i) & (ii) only
☐ (i) & (iii) only
☐ (ii) & (iii) only
☐ (i), (ii), & (iii)

8.8 **Which one of the following should be excluded when analysing customer account profitability?**

☐ Sales revenue
☐ Direct product costs
☐ Allocation of fixed overheads
☐ Sales force costs specific to the customer

8.9 **Which of the following is associated with 'transactional' rather than 'relationship' marketing?**

☐ Quality is regarded as a concern of the entire organisation
☐ Regular communication
☐ Commitment to remaining competitive above all
☐ High levels of customer commitment and service

8.10 "A set of controllable variables that marketing managers have at their disposal to affect the sales and fortunes of each of the company's products or services."

Which element of marketing does this statement describe?

☐ Marketing mix
☐ Marketing research
☐ Marketing segmentation
☐ Marketing orientation

8.11 The Directors of X Co are concerned that the company's share price has fallen significantly in recent weeks, as analysts have been advising investors to sell shares in the company.

The Directors are surprised about why the analysts are giving this advice, as X is going to comfortably exceed its profit forecast for the year. However, the PR Director admitted that the last update he gave to the analysts didn't make this clear.

In relation to Payne's six markets model, which market does this demonstrate X has a weakness in?

- ☐ Customer markets
- ☐ Influence markets
- ☐ Recruitment markets
- ☐ Referral markets

9 Organisational change

9.1 XP is a company which provides financial advice to its clients. In recent years, the Board of XP has recognised the need to continually develop the range of services it offers. The Board has always encouraged collaboration and partnerships with other organisations to develop and enhance the services it offers, and to utilise the expertise and knowledge of other organisations. XP's management has also been highly innovative in the services it provides. It regularly analyses and keeps up to date with changes in the environment in which it operates. XP operates a sophisticated website to promote its services and keep in touch with its clients.

Which of the following attributes of XP make it a change adept organisation?

Select all that apply.

- ☐ XP attempts to respond to competitors' strategic changes
- ☐ The Board of XP encourages collaboration and partnerships with other organisations
- ☐ XP's management has always been highly innovative in the services it provides
- ☐ XP regularly analyses changes in its environment
- ☐ XP operates a sophisticated website to promote its services and keep in touch with its clients

9.2 Z is a power generating company in Country H. Z's customers are increasingly concerned with the level of emissions resulting from the power generation process and are willing to switch to suppliers who are able to demonstrate that they use renewable sources as part of their energy mix. The Government of H is more in favour of nuclear energy as a way of reducing carbon emissions.

The new managing director of Z is a strong supporter of tidal and solar energy, and wishes to build several solar farms in the next couple of years. However, these farms are not popular with local residents, who have used their influence at a local level to obstruct planning permission applications. The Government of H has encountered similar problems with pushing through its nuclear ambitions, and has now published plans to allow large scale projects to be centrally approved without the need for as much local consultation.

Identify whether each of the following are driving or restraining forces in relation to Z's desire to invest in solar farms.

Current planning application process in Country H	☐ Driving Force	☐ Restraining Force
Z's customers	☐ Driving Force	☐ Restraining Force
New managing director	☐ Driving Force	☐ Restraining Force
Proposed planning laws	☐ Driving Force	☐ Restraining Force
Local residents	☐ Driving Force	☐ Restraining Force

9.3 Which of the following feature in the McKinsey 7S model of organisational elements?

Select all that apply.

☐ Shared values
☐ Stories
☐ Strategy
☐ Staff
☐ Symbols
☐ Software

9.4 People generally do not like change. Comfortable routines have to be altered and there is no guarantee at the outset that the new system will work as well as, let alone better than, the old one.

Kurt Lewin developed a programme of planned change and improved performance, involving the management of a three-stage process of behaviour modification. One of the stages is mainly concerned with identifying what the new desirable behaviour should be, communicating it, and encouraging individuals and groups to 'own' the new behaviour.

Which of the following stages in Lewin's model does this describe?

☐ Unfreezing
☐ Culture change
☐ Change
☐ Refreezing

9.5 You are the manager of a department that is in the process of introducing a new shift system. There has been some resistance to this change from the employees in the department.

How can you most effectively change the employees' attitude to the change and gain acceptance of it?

☐ Pay the employees to accept the change.

☐ Get team leaders to instruct others on the benefits of the change.

☐ Present the change to the employees as 'a done deal' and emphasise the fact that there is nothing you can do, much as you want to.

☐ Tell the employees the change is for a 'trial period' and hope they get used to it.

9.6 KYJ is a charity supporting sporting excellence in children between the ages of 12 – 18. The parents of children working with KYJ value its traditional approaches to coaching, which have remained largely unchanged over the last 20 years.

However, KYJ's trustees have been warned by the Charities' Regulator that KYJ will need to modernise if it wishes to retain its charitable status in the coming years. Loss of charitable status would leave KYJ unable to access government grants which it relies upon to fund 80% of its budgetary needs

None of KYJ's management or staff has a clear vision of its future role, nor a clear idea of what it needs to do to 'move with the times'. Management and staff are loyal to KYJ and wish to be consulted on the development of KYJ.

Which one of the following approaches to change should KYJ adopt?

☐ Identify a Champion of Change from within KYJ to lead change
☐ Encourage a member of KYJ's management to act as a Change Leader
☐ Appoint a Change Agent to develop KYJ
☐ Engage a team of consultants to instruct KYJ's management on its future direction

---

9.7 Pear has recently developed a portable music player, which it has designed and marketed exclusively itself. The new device enables users to shop for, download, browse, and listen to music via wireless networking. The introduction of the device was a transformational change which was forced upon Pear due to the changing competitive environment in the book sales market where it previously earned the majority of its revenue. This development and introduction of the new device occurred over a period of only one year.

Which of the following forms of organisational change best categorises the initial development and introduction of the portable music player by Pear?

☐   Evolution

☐   Revolution

☐   Adaptation

☐   Reconstruction

9.8 Triggers for change can either be internal or external.

Which of the following are external triggers?

Select all the apply.

☐   Changes in economic conditions such as the onset of a recession

☐   The arrival of a new CEO joining the organisation

☐   Changes in customer tastes and expectations

☐   Relocation of a business unit a new country

☐   A new competitor entering the market

9.9 In recent months, the Directors of PBB Co have become concerned that the company's net profits have fallen behind target. Two separate initiatives have been proposed to try to help improve PBB's profits:

(i)   Senior management have identified a number of potential redundancies across the company which could be made in order to reduce costs

(ii)   Managers have been encouraging their staff to suggest improvements and share knowledge, to ensure PBB makes best use of ideas from staff throughout the company

In relation to Boer and Nohria's 'Theory E' and 'Theory O' approaches to change management, which of the proposed initiatives is/are consistent with a Theory O approach?

☐   Neither of them

☐   (i) only

☐   (ii) only

☐   Both of them

9.10 Successful acquisitions or mergers should result in synergies.

Which one of the following best describes synergies?

☐   Gaining economies of scale

☐   The combined entities are worth more together than apart

☐   Increases in revenue as a result of gaining new customers

☐   Reductions in headcount

10 Leading and managing change

10.1 PPI is a state-owned monopoly provider of power generation in Country J. Under international trade regulations, the Government of J has been instructed to open up its power generation industry to foreign competition within one year, which is a very short timescale indeed in this context. The Government would also need to stop subsidising PPI at that time.

PPI is currently subsidised by the Government of J, but this will not be lawful once the market is opened up to new competitors. In order to reduce PPI's reliance on public subsidies it will be necessary to reduce the employee headcount and alter current pension entitlements. To date, both of these initiatives have been resisted by operative staff. The operative staff of PPI are all members of the same trade union, whilst members of management belong to a separate trade union.

The Government of J has decided that the only way to ensure PPI becomes competitive is to sell it to private sector investors. But first it needs to make PPI profitable.

Select the THREE change strategies from the list below which are most suitable for PPI's management to adopt in these circumstances.

☐ Education and communication: introduce a programme of workplace meetings to help management to win workers' support for change by explaining the forces that threaten PPI to staff, the restructuring and redundancies it plans

☐ Explicit and implicit coercion: policies of forced economies, redundancies and closures to reduce costs, and the introduction of changes to working practices

☐ Participation and involvement: management and operative staff work together to identify efficiency gains and new markets to make PPI profitable

☐ Negotiation and agreement: urgent meetings with trade union representatives to develop a plan to make PPI profitable and to incentivise employees by offering them a share in the profits of PPI when it is sold

☐ Facilitation and support: announcement of generous financial packages and help with finding new jobs for staff who are willing to volunteer for redundancy from PPI, and provision of training to those staff willing to change job roles

10.2 DH is a Chief Financial Officer (CFO) and wishes to develop her change leadership skills to support strategic change in her organisation. Inspection of DH's diary shows that she spends her work time engaged in a range of activities.

Select the activities below that are essential to effective change leadership by a CFO.

Select all that apply.

☐ Planning and budgeting for the future of the organisation
☐ Setting a direction for the organisation
☐ Controlling and problem-solving during the implementation of strategy
☐ Aligning people by communicating the direction of the strategy
☐ Motivating and inspiring staff to pursue the organisation's vision

10.3 **From the following list, identify the elements that help to make up the culture of an organisation.**

Select all that apply.

☐ Beliefs and values
☐ Customs
☐ Symbols
☐ Ownership
☐ Technology

10.4 **Which of the following could cause change to fail?**

Select all that apply.

- ☐ Vision is clearly developed
- ☐ Vision is poorly communicated
- ☐ Creation of short-term wins
- ☐ Systems, policies and skills are not aligned
- ☐ Change is not perceived as urgent
- ☐ Powerful guiding coalition

10.5 Johnson, Scholes and Whittington identified five styles of change management.

Which one of these styles of change management is most likely to be undertaken by a change agent?

- ☐ Education and communication
- ☐ Collaboration/participation
- ☐ Intervention
- ☐ Direction
- ☐ Coercion/edict

10.6 KNG is a technology company that was founded by three software engineers about fifteen years ago. The founders, who are still directors of the company, have consistently sought to create an innovative environment at KNG. They are always looking to test new ideas and find new solutions, and they have encouraged their staff to also be similarly inquisitive and curious. Experimentation is valued within the company, because the founders believe that the company can learn through experimentation even if the individual experiments themselves are unsuccessful.

Which of the following leadership styles, identified by Reardon and Rowe, best describe those being employed at KNG?

- ☐ Commanding
- ☐ Inspirational
- ☐ Logical
- ☐ Supportive

10.7 CC is an advertising agency, which has a customer relationship management system (CRMS) based on a software package it bought several years ago. However, CC's marketing staff believe that the inadequacies in its current CRMS are resulting in CC being left behind by its competitors. The marketing staff believe that the company should implement a new CRMS, giving CC the customer information it needs to survive in a highly competitive market.

CC could purchase the industry standard CRMS, which could be expensive but is well proven. Some of CC's marketing staff have previously used this CRMS in other companies, and believe it would benefit CC considerably. The software supplier guarantees to have it operational within three months of purchase. However, P, CC's IT director, has stated that although he and the IT Department are aware of the limitations of the current CRMS, he would be very resistant to this change. P has stated that a 'Big Bang' change to CC's CRMS would be too disruptive.

Select the most appropriate action to overcome P's resistance to the immediate purchase of the new CRMS:

☐ Communication and education: P needs to be convinced that the limitations of the existing software package are a serious constraint upon CC

☐ Facilitation and support: P must be reassured that his personal position will not be jeopardised

☐ Participation and involvement: the trigger for change has not come from P, but the implementation of the change will benefit from the active participation and involvement of P and the IT staff

☐ Manipulation and co-optation: as the change needs to happen immediately P should be offered incentives to agree to the change

10.8 **Which one of the following correctly describes a change recipient?**

☐ Someone who proposes the change
☐ Someone who legitimises the change
☐ Someone who implements the change
☐ Someone who must adapt to the change

10.9 The Directors at PHL Co are concerned that the poor quality of information they can get from the company's marketing information system is causing it to lag behind its competitors and lose customers.

The Directors want to introduce a new marketing information system as quickly as possible, but are concerned that none of the managers at PHL have any experience of such a project.

Therefore they have chosen to use an external consultant, who has experience of working on similar projects, as an external change agent.

In relation to PHL, which of the following is/are advantages of using an external change agent?

(i) The agent can bring capabilities and skills which PHL's managers don't currently have

(ii) The agent can draw on their experience from working with other organisations to recommend best practice for PHL's project

☐ Neither of them
☐ (i) only
☐ (ii) only
☐ Both of them

10.10 Johnson, Scholes and Whittington suggest the cultural web model can be used to gain an understanding of an organisation's culture and therefore the way its members behave and how its strategy develops.

Which one of the following is not one of the manifestations of culture included in the web?

☐ Symbols
☐ Power structures
☐ Staff
☐ Control systems

10.11 **Which of the following are elements of Tom Peters' concept of 'Thriving on Chaos'?**

Select all that apply.

☐ Successful companies encourage constant innovation
☐ Continuous change does not alter the underlying strategy of an organisation
☐ Companies need the flexibility to be able to respond quickly to changes in the environment
☐ Leaders need to have a clear vision of what they want to achieve

10.12 LBP is a training company, providing a range of courses to young professionals. Six months ago, the directors of LBP recognised that the need for a change in the company's strategy, following the entry of two new competitors into the market. A project team (made up of senior managers from across the company) was assembled to develop a new strategy, and the team quickly identified that LBP needed to offer more of its courses online, rather than concentrating on face-to-face tuition.

The members of the project team discussed the new proposals with the members of their departments, and how the new strategy would affect them.

Three months after introducing the online courses, the CEO announced that LBP had already achieved its budgeted number of online students for the first year, so the whole company should be very proud of this, and the annual staff bonuses would reflect this. However, six months later, the number of new students had halved, following negative feedback from students who had been unable to access their courses properly due to problems with LBP's IT systems.

According to Kotter's model of the eight stages of change leadership, which step had LBP failed to meet?

☐ Creating a guiding coalition
☐ Creating short-term wins
☐ Communicating the vision
☐ Empowering others to act on the vision

10.13 **Which of the following are included in the power skills which Kanter identified that change agents need in order to help them overcome resistance to change in an organisation?**

Select all that apply.

☐ Visible support from senior management
☐ Willingness to stake personal rewards on results being achieved
☐ Self-confidence tempered with humility
☐ Recommending best practice approaches, based on prior experience
☐ An ability to collaborate effectively
☐ An ability to bring a fresh perspective to a change initiative

11 Strategic performance management

11.1 All strategic planning models and performance measurement systems have limitations that must be considered when deciding how to apply them in any organisation.

Below are two limitations of a particular model of strategic analysis:

- It is more applicable to manufacturing industries than service industries
- It requires an extensive re-working of accounting information to support it

Which model do these limitations relate to?

☐ Kaplan and Norton's Balanced Scorecard
☐ The Boston Consulting Group's Portfolio Matrix
☐ Porter's Value Chain Analysis
☐ Ansoff's Product Market Growth Matrix

11.2 JK is a manufacturer and installer of domestic boilers. Until recently, its business model was based on selling a standard boiler, brand name 'Basic', with a very limited degree of customer choice, at low profit margins. JK manufactures and installs 25,000 'Basic' boilers a year. The average revenue per 'Basic' boiler is $2,000.

Two years ago, JK launched a new boiler, brand name 'Deluxe'. This boiler is aimed at high net-worth customers and it offers a very large degree of choice for the customer, and makes use of the highest standards of materials. A 'Deluxe' boiler retails for an average price of $8,000. Currently, JK installs an average 2,000 Deluxe boilers each year.

In the next year, JK aims to increase market share in both areas of its business. JK's business is generated from repeat orders, word of mouth recommendations, and local press advertising.

From the list below, select the critical success factors (CSFs) for JK which would assist in it achieving its business aim for the next year.

Select all that apply.

- ☐   Market share growth
- ☐   Brand performance
- ☐   Quality of manufacturing
- ☐   Customers' satisfaction levels

11.3 **What are the four perspectives of Kaplan & Norton's balanced scorecard?**

- ☐   Financial; customer; internal business; productivity
- ☐   Financial; customer; innovation and learning; internal business
- ☐   Business; financial; innovation and learning; quality
- ☐   Customer; quality; external effectiveness; internal efficiency

---

11.4 The strategy map which Kaplan & Norton developed as an extension to the balanced scorecard illustrates that there is a hierarchy among the four perspectives of the scorecard.

According to the strategy map, which is the highest level perspective in the scorecard?

- ☐   Customer
- ☐   Financial
- ☐   Innovation and learning
- ☐   Internal business

11.5 Kaplan and Norton's balanced scorecard approach includes financial indicators, and proposes three other categories, or perspectives, for measuring performance.

Which TWO of the following criteria are NOT derived from the perspectives of the balanced scorecard?

- ☐   Intellectual assets and organisational learning
- ☐   Future strategic potential
- ☐   Customer satisfaction
- ☐   Office efficiency
- ☐   Present competitive position

11.6 EAV is a retailer of electrical equipment. As part of the performance management process, EAV's senior management team identifies objectives and critical success factors (CSFs) and then sets targets for store managers to motivate them to achieve results in line with the company's objectives and goals.

From the list below, select the most appropriate KPI and target for two of EAV's CSFs: customer satisfaction, and growth in sales revenue.

- Increase in market share
- 3% increase in like-for-like sales
- 50% of shoppers return annually
- Number of repeat customers

CSF	KPI	Target
Customer satisfaction		
Growth in sales revenue		

11.7 TRV manufactures automobiles which are sold at the high-priced end of the market to discerning customers who value extreme handling and performance.

TRV has a mission statement that emphasises meeting its Corporate Social Responsibilities (CSR). It also devotes considerable investment into developing new technologies that will improve the performance of its vehicles.

Despite its differentiated position in the market, TRV still suffers from low profit margins due to its high production costs and a general decline in the prices of high-performance cars due to foreign competition from more efficient producers.

Which of the following would be the most appropriate Critical Success Factors for TRV?

Select all that apply.

☐ Awareness amongst performance car buyers of the superior performance of TRV's vehicles
☐ Annual reductions in the production costs of TRV's vehicles
☐ Superior comfort of TRVs automobiles
☐ Superior reputation for CSR compared to foreign luxury car makers
☐ Superior performance of TRV's vehicles compared to its domestic and foreign rivals

11.8 **Which one of the balanced scorecard perspectives examines an organisation's success in developing new products, for example by looking at the number of new products developed?**

☐ Financial
☐ Customer
☐ Innovation and learning
☐ Internal business process

11.9 Which of the following statements about the performance pyramid (developed by Lynch and Cross) are true?

(i)   The pyramid focuses on a range of objectives for external effectiveness and internal efficiency.

(ii)   The pyramid encourages organisations to look at performance measures in relation to a wide range of stakeholder groups, such as customers, employees and suppliers.

(iii)   The hierarchical levels of the pyramid encourage operational performance measures to be linked to strategic goals.

☐   (i) and (ii) only
☐   (i) and (iii) only
☐   (ii) and (iii) only
☐   (i), (ii) and (iii)

11.10 The senior managers of a company are keen to encourage innovation and they have drawn up some goals to encourage staff to look for new markets, products, processes and designs to improve productivity.

Which three on the list below are likely to achieve their purpose?

☐   Ensure that senior managers welcome, and are seen to welcome, changes for the better.
☐   Introduce more bureaucratic structures to foster interactive feedback.
☐   Understand people in the organisation and their needs.
☐   Recognise and encourage potential entrepreneurs.
☐   Switch to short term horizons that encourage innovation.

11.11 F Co has used Fitzgerald & Moon's 'Building Block' model as the basis of its performance measurements system for the first time this year.

As F Co is a service company, its directors felt that the model was appropriate for it, and could help to improve its performance. However, performance has continued to fall this year, and some of the factors contributing to this are listed below.

Identify whether these factors relate to dimensions, standards or rewards in the Building Block model.

A number of employees have said that they weren't sure what their objectives were, or what goals they were working towards.

☐   Dimensions
☐   Standards
☐   Rewards

Employees have given up trying to reach their bonus targets because they feel they are neither achievable nor fair.

☐   Dimensions
☐   Standards
☐   Rewards

Customer satisfaction surveys have shown a decline in the reliability and responsiveness of the service customers have received from F's staff.

☐   Dimensions
☐   Standards
☐   Rewards

12 Performance measurement

12.1 KP manufactures and sells a range of cosmetics in its home country. It has four business divisions. Data for the most recent year (20X3), and comparative market growth rates for the preceding year (20X2) are available.

Division	Sales Revenue 20X3 $m	Profit (Loss) 20X3 $m	Market Share
E	867	126	4%
F	1,796	468	30%
G	42	(17)	18%
H	963	187	52%
Total Group	3,668	764	

Division	Market share of largest rival	Market growth rate 20X3	Market growth rate 20X2
E	60%	0%	0%
F	19%	8%	10%
G	22%	38%	23%
H	42%	18%	25%

Which of the following strategic options should KP investigate first?

☐ Selling Division G to eliminate losses

☐ Buying a rival to Division H, to acquire its market share of 6%

☐ Investing in Division F to increase its market share

☐ Divesting Division E to a rival firm in the same market

12.2 Traditional management accounting focuses on providing information to assist decisions at operational and managerial levels, and to monitor performance at these levels. Strategic management accounting provides additional information.

Which of the following pieces of information would be more likely to be provided by strategic management accountants, rather than by a set of traditional management accounts?

Select all that apply.

☐ Investment appraisals

☐ Long term forecasts of market trends

☐ Flexed budgets

☐ Competitor prices and profit margins

☐ Assessments of potential acquisition targets

12.3 Residual income (RI) has been proven to be theoretically superior to return on investment (ROI) as a performance measure, but ROI is still more popular in practice.

Which of the following is most likely to be a reason for ROI retaining popularity?

☐ It encourages goal congruence

☐ Cost of capital is difficult to calculate

☐ Profit can be easily manipulated

☐ It can account for different levels of risk

12.4 **Which of the following factors make it harder to monitor the performance of divisions in a multinational group, compared to monitoring the performance of divisions which are all based in the same country?**

Select all that apply.

- ☐ Differing legal frameworks in the different countries
- ☐ Different cultures
- ☐ Economic conditions in the different countries
- ☐ Transfer pricing
- ☐ Decentralised management structure in the group

12.5 The usefulness of profit as a single control measure has been criticised in recent years.

Which of the following is NOT a reason to support this criticism?

- ☐ Profit can be easily manipulated
- ☐ Profit provides a narrow focus for performance measurement
- ☐ Profit measurement alone can lead to short termism
- ☐ Profit is simple for managers to understand

12.6 S is a listed company that manufactures heavy machinery. It comprises two divisions of the same age, with identical equipment, that conduct identical business activities in different parts of the same country. Both are considering installing a new machine. Divisional managers receive bonuses if they are able to increase ROI year-on-year.

Data for the divisions, and the machine, are as follows:

	Division A	Division B
Current ROI	18%	7%
Cost of Capital	11%	11%
NPV of proposed machine	$104m	($3m)
ROI of proposed machine	15%	12%

Which of the following pieces of advice should be given to the senior management of S?

Select all that apply.

- ☐ The manager of Division B has an incentive to invest in the new machine which would be against the interest of shareholders
- ☐ The use of ROI is encouraging both divisional managers not to invest in the new machine because it doesn't repay in the short term
- ☐ The manager of Division A has an incentive to invest in the new machine which would be against the interest of shareholders
- ☐ The managerial bonus system is rewarding poor performance by the manager of Division B
- ☐ ROI is an unsuitable measure for evaluating new investments

---

12.7 Return on investment can be used to assess the performance of strategic business units and, by extension, that of their managers.

Which of the following formulae would be used to calculate return on investment for a SBU?

- ☐ Profit before interest and tax/Operations capital employed
- ☐ Net profit/Shareholders' capital employed
- ☐ Profit before interest and tax/Shareholders' capital employed
- ☐ Net profit/Operations capital employed

12.8 ARC is a manufacturing company. In the past, shareholders had been critical of the company's performance measurement systems, arguing that they encouraged ARC's managers to focus on short term profits rather than the amount of wealth the company is creating for shareholders.

In response to these criticisms, ARC has introduced a new performance measurement system, in which marketing expenditure and product development costs are added back to profit on the grounds that they will generate value for the business in future periods.

Which of the following performance measurement systems is ARC using now?

☐ Return on Capital Employed
☐ Economic Value Added
☐ Shareholder value analysis
☐ Total shareholder return

12.9 **Which TWO of the following are benefits of decentralisation?**

☐ Greater speed of decision making
☐ Better crisis management
☐ It improves the motivation of junior managers
☐ Decisions are made at one place in the organisation
☐ Reductions in bureaucracy

12.10 RST Co is currently evaluating a proposal to design and launch a major new product range. The Finance Director has suggested that in order to maximise the value the range generates for RST's shareholders, its performance should be managed in a way which is consistent with a shareholder value analysis (SVA) approach.

Which of the following are consistent with an SVA approach?

Select all that apply.

☐ Research and development costs should be added back when calculating operating profits generated by the range.

☐ The range should be designed in a way which maximises its useful life.

☐ Inventory levels as a percentage of sales revenue from the products should be kept as low as possible.

☐ The value of intangible assets created by the range, such as brand name and goodwill, should be included in the project evaluation.

☐ The operating profit margin the products earn should be maximised, either by increasing sales prices or by reducing costs.

13 Mixed Bank 1

13.1 **Which of the following best describes a non-market strategy?**

☐ Non-market strategy is the alternative name for the sort of strategies pursued by a Not For Profit Organisation (NPO).

☐ A strategy that focuses on developing an organisation's core competences and leveraging them to achieve competitive advantage in new markets.

☐ A strategy that seeks to maintain relationships with governments, media, regulators and society at large to achieve sustainable advantage.

☐ Aggressive strategies by rivals aimed at undermining the business by depriving it of key resources instead of competing for its customers.

13.2 A CIMA member was asked to describe an ethical problem they encountered at work and the steps they took to deal with it. They wrote the following account:

'My manager asked me to provide a report to justify a decision to outsource the cleaning of my firm's offices to a particular contractor. I know, from conversations with him, that my manager has a financial interest in that contractor. I wrote a report justifying the decision to outsource to the contractor as I was instructed but, to cover myself, I clipped a note to the hard copy of the report stating that I did not personally agree with the findings or conclusions of my report because I had not shown professional competence or due care when constructing it.'

Which of the following indicates this member's understanding of events?

☐ EXCELLENT: they have defined the ethical principles correctly and the action they took to resolve it was appropriate and effective.

☐ GOOD: they recognised and understood the ethical principles involved but the action they took was not strong enough in the circumstances.

☐ POOR: they did not understand the ethical principles involved correctly and the action they took was not strong enough in the circumstances.

☐ VERY POOR: the person who wrote this has failed to recognise that ethical issues are involved and has made no attempt to address them.

13.3 **Which one of the following factors associated with international trade would be the most appropriate to classify under the 'P' heading in the 'PEST' model?**

☐ Shipping costs and insurance
☐ Legislative treaties and increased governmental risk
☐ Economic development and government grants
☐ Social customs and educational levels

13.4 **When deciding whether to continue or cease production of an unprofitable product, which of the following factors should you consider?**

1. Contribution per unit of limiting factor
2. Existence of complementary products
3. Strategic value of remaining in the market
4. Allocation of fixed overhead

☐ (1) only
☐ (2) and (3) only
☐ (1), (2) and (3) only
☐ All of the factors (1) – (4)

13.5 A management skills training company buys the printing company that converts their loose-leaf manuals into course textbooks.

This is an example of which sort of diversification?

☐ Unrelated diversification
☐ Related horizontal diversification
☐ Related vertical forward diversification
☐ Related vertical backward diversification

13.6 **Identify whether each of the following statements is true or false.**

Information systems determine corporate / business strategy	☐	True	☐	False
Information systems support corporate / business strategy	☐	True	☐	False

 BPP LEARNING MEDIA

13.7 TUV is a global operator of movie rental shops. Customers visit TUV stores to rent discs of movies for five nights at a fixed price to take home and watch, then return them.

WXY is a new business that operates an online service in which films are licensed from the copyright owner and provided to WXY's members to watch online, in return for a low monthly fee.

Select the MOST likely explanation for the falling profits of TUV from the list below.

☐ Falling profits are the effect of increased market entry.
☐ Falling profits are the effect of increased power of substitutes.
☐ Falling profits are the effect of increased competitive rivalry.
☐ Falling profits are the effect of increased buyer power.

13.8 **Which one of the following correctly describes the first stage of Lewin's three stage model of change?**

☐ Provide and sell a motive or reason to change
☐ Change all existing behaviours
☐ Move to the desired state
☐ Consolidate the change

13.9 **The democratic leadership style works best when:**

☐ The team needs to buy into, or has ownership of, a decision, plan or strategic change
☐ The team needs a new vision because circumstances have changed
☐ The team needs to rebuild trust due to stress or rapid change
☐ There is a crisis situation

13.10 BLUPA is a private health company operating a not-for-profit business model. BLUPA reinvests all of its surplus funds back into its facilities, staff and research. It uses the Balanced Scorecard to monitor and evaluate the performance of its hospitals and departments. It presently collects data on the following four Key Performance Indicators (KPIs):

1. Average time between patient arrival and attention by a member of medical staff
2. Average cost per patient admission
3. Errors in medical records keeping per 100 admissions
4. Percentage of patients expressing satisfaction with BLUPA's service

Which of the following perspectives is NOT represented in the Key Performance Indicators monitored by BLUPA?

☐ Customer
☐ Internal business process
☐ Financial
☐ Innovation and learning

14 Mixed Bank 2

14.1 **In which of the following situations would you recommend the adoption of a rational (traditional) approach to strategy formulation?**

Select all that apply.

☐ Management needs to improve profits in the short term.
☐ Management has a high degree of comfort with the techniques of the rational approach.
☐ The future can be forecast with reasonable certainty.
☐ The organisation needs to innovate and to think creatively.
☐ In an organisation where departmental loyalties take priority over attaining corporate goals.

14.2 PHY is a contractor that develops and sells medical diagnostic equipment such as scanners and monitors. This equipment helps provide early identification and treatment of life-threatening conditions and injuries, but can also be used to help non-critical work such as enhancing appearance through cosmetic surgery.

Which item below raises the LEAST challenge to the business ethics of PHY?

☐ The higher prices charged to developing countries for its medical diagnostic equipment compared to the prices charged to developed economies.

☐ Negative impacts on patients from inaccuracies in its medical diagnostic equipment.

☐ The use of its equipment by hospitals to enhance appearance as well as to assist in curing illness and injury.

☐ Poor pay and working conditions of employees and suppliers engaged in making medical diagnostic equipment for PHY.

14.3 There are three types of 'real option' relevant to strategic projects.

Which option is best deployed in a situation where expected revenue streams don't materialise?

☐ The option to make follow-on investments
☐ The option to abandon a project
☐ The option to wait
☐ The option to evaluate a project

14.4 Terry's manager is interested in benchmarking and has asked Terry to find out what he can about it. In particular, the manager needs to be able to stress the advantages of benchmarking when he puts forward his proposals at the next heads of departments' meeting.

Which of the following would Terry choose to tell his manager are benefits of benchmarking?

Select all that apply.

☐ The comparisons are carried out by outside consultants who do not have to live with any changes implemented as a result of the exercise

☐ It will guarantee improvements in operations

☐ It can provide an early warning of future problems

☐ It may generate new ideas from which all participants benefit

☐ It focuses on improvement in key areas and sets targets, which are challenging but 'achievable'

14.5 Christine Ltd is considering a project with the following revenue stream:

Year	Investment $000	Variable costs $000	Sales $000	Net cash flows $000
0	(20,000)			
1		(7,000)	18,000	11,000
2		(7,000)	18,000	11,000
3		(7,000)	18,000	11,000

The company's cost of capital is 8%.

Assuming the project has a three year life-span, by what percentage will the aggregate net cash flows from years 1 to 3 have to fall for the project to produce a zero net present value?

☐ 18.0%
☐ 29.4%
☐ 41.7%
☐ 46.3%

14.6 **Which of the following are likely to be consequences of NOT having an IT strategy.**

Select all that apply.

- ☐ An organisation's IT costs escalate
- ☐ Business-led systems are developed
- ☐ IT is exploited to gain competitive advantage
- ☐ Systems may not be integrated
- ☐ Poor quality information is produced

14.7 Most of the components in a B computer are made by other companies, whilst B focuses on its strengths of marketing and customer support and integration of the components into the final computer products. The process involved in making, selling and delivering a B computer to a customer includes a B customer service representative; an assembly line and assembly crew; suppliers for various components; and the delivery truck and driver who delivers the computer to the customer's home. However, to the customer, B appears a single, seamless organisation; and when a customer places and order, the information from this order is automatically passed on to B's suppliers via an electronic data interchange system.

The organisation of B is best described as an example of:

- ☐ Outsourcing
- ☐ A virtual organisation
- ☐ Customer Relationship Management
- ☐ A learning organisation

14.8 The Gemini 4Rs framework suggests that for a change process to be successful, 4Rs must be present.

Which of the following is NOT a stage in the 4Rs framework?

- ☐ Reframing
- ☐ Rescoping
- ☐ Restructuring
- ☐ Revitalising
- ☐ Renewal

14.9 NE is the CEO of ZBH, a hospital in a major city. One year ago NE initiated a radical change initiative to "fundamentally rethink the way in which ZBH serves our customers":

NE laid down "Three Guiding Principles":

1. Patients are not problems, they are people with problems
2. Bring the expertise to the patient, don't depend on the patient to find the expertise
3. Learn what we need to do, don't just do what we have learned

NE encouraged the department and managers of ZBH to form working groups to interpret these 'Three Guiding Principles' and to implement them as appropriate in their areas of responsibility.

A year after launching the radical change initiative NE is disappointed. He complains that very little has been accomplished and that he is constantly having to spend time with managers urging more progress and suggesting ways in which they could apply the 'Three Guiding Principles' to their areas of responsibility.

Managers and staff at ZBH have commented that working groups were initially exciting and well-attended but that after a few months they had lots of ideas but they didn't know if they were appropriate, and they didn't have any plans or resources to implement them. This led staff to become discouraged and to criticise NE and the radical change initiative.

Which of the following roles of change leadership did NE fail to perform properly?

Select all that apply.

☐ Initiate change
☐ Communicate a vision
☐ Energise teams
☐ Support the change process
☐ Advocate progress

14.10 The Building Block Model devised by Fitzgerald and Moon set out a framework for the design and analysis of performance management systems. The 'Standards' building block has three sub-components.

Which of the following are components of the 'Standards' building block in Fitzgerald and Moon's performance management model?

Select all that apply.

☐ Innovative
☐ Equitable
☐ Flexible
☐ Achievable
☐ Owned

---

15 Mixed Bank 3

15.1 In the movie industry, a film producer acts a route to gaining finance for the film by investing in it and encouraging others in invest. A film director is responsible for delivering the vision of the film by directing and filming the action and for ensuring it is delivered within budget.

Which of the following analogies describes the proper exercise of corporate governance in the strategic management of the business by the Board of a large publically-quoted corporation?

☐ The role of Non-Executive Directors is to be like film producers and the role of Executive Directors is to be like film directors.

☐ The role of all Directors is to be like film directors.

☐ The role of all Directors is to be like film producers.

☐ The role of a Company Director combines some of the role of film producers with some of the role of film directors.

15.2 Some organisations may decide to establish an internal group of experts, which is then referred to internally as a 'think tank'. A think tank is considered by many organisations to be a useful intuitive forecasting method which places emphasis upon the knowledge and judgement of a group of experts rather than on statistical forecasting methods.

Which of the following are features of a think tank?

Select all that apply.

☐ Members speculate about the future and are asked to provide subjective probabilities about their predictions.

☐ Employees from all levels of the organisation and with varying levels of expertise meet and propose answers to an initial single question posed by a session leader.

☐ The removal of positional authority in the group to enable free discussion to take place.

☐ The independence of members enables unpopular or novel ideas to be discussed.

☐ Its group nature facilitates the sharing of knowledge and encourages a shared view.

15.3 Which forecasting method involves a number of experts independently and anonymously giving their opinions and insights on a particular trend and how it may develop, with the ultimate aim of reaching a consensus?

☐ Cross-impact analysis
☐ Scenario planning
☐ Game theory
☐ Delphi technique

15.4 In Porter's value chain which of the following is a support activity?

☐ Operations
☐ Marketing and sales
☐ After-sales service
☐ Procurement

15.5 Differentiation will be less effective as a competitive tool in which of the following situations?

1. The market becomes price sensitive
2. The difference isn't communicated to the customer
3. The cost leader gains a further cost advantage
4. The difference is protected by patent

☐ (1) only
☐ (1) and (2) only
☐ (2) and (4) only
☐ (1), (3) and (4)

15.6 Which of the following are reasons why an organisation needs an information technology (IT) strategy?

Select all that apply.

☐ IT is best left to the technical department.
☐ The success of business depends on the quality of the information in the organisation.
☐ IT does not effect everyone in the organisation.
☐ IT can provide the organisation with the competitive advantage needed for commercial success.
☐ IT is not a capital investment, but an expense.

15.7 AAA is a manufacturer that operates e-procurement as part of its approach to Supply Chain Management (SCM). It also builds partnerships with its suppliers.

Which of the following describe benefits that AAA may enjoy from e-procurement?

Select all that apply.

- ☐ Reduction in the transaction costs of dealing with suppliers.
- ☐ Ability for AAA to constantly shop around a range of suppliers to buy inputs more cheaply.
- ☐ Higher production and sales due to suppliers responding quickly to demand and leading to fewer stock outs of components.
- ☐ Lower inventory holding costs, because the reduced cost of placing and processing orders means AAA can place orders more frequently.
- ☐ Reduction in the risk that unauthorised purchases will be made.

15.8 **According to Kotter and Schlesinger, which of the following are suitable approaches for dealing with resistance to change?**

Select all that apply.

- ☐ Education and communication
- ☐ Participation and involvement
- ☐ Networking and support
- ☐ Mutual co-operation
- ☐ Negotiation and agreement

15.9 **Which TWO of the following are key characteristics of an effective team?**

- ☐ An effective team must be led by a democratic team leader.
- ☐ An effective team has a unity of purpose, and all team members understand this purpose.
- ☐ An effective team involves its stakeholders in assessing progress towards goals.
- ☐ An effective team avoids conflict and disagreement between team members.

15.10 Service Co is a service company, and it uses a range of performance measures based on the 'Results and Determinants' framework (the 'Building Block' model).

The senior managers at Service Co have recently been focusing on measures which look at reliability, responsiveness, courtesy, competence and availability.

Which determinant are the managers most interested in?

- ☐ Competitive performance
- ☐ Resource utilisation
- ☐ Financial performance
- ☐ Quality of service

16 Mixed Bank 4

16.1 V is a well established, mid-priced airline business. It is currently considering setting up a 'no-frills', low fare subsidiary of its business.

Which THREE of the following activities would take place within the strategic analysis phase of V's strategic planning process?

☐ Evaluation of the competitors' actions
☐ Evaluation of how new staff would be recruited and trained
☐ Evaluation of which planes to use
☐ Evaluation of forecast passenger volumes
☐ Evaluation of public concern for environmental damage

16.2 **How does setting objectives relate to the mission statement of an organisation?**

☐ The mission states what the objectives are
☐ The mission gives managers a focus for setting objectives
☐ The mission has nothing to do with setting objectives
☐ The mission is decided after setting the objectives

16.3 **Which of the following statements is/are true?**

(i) Game theory highlights the importance of competitor analysis, and of having an insight into competitors' strategies.

(ii) Game theory provides useful guidance about how an organisation can implement any co-operative strategies it develops with competitors.

☐ Neither of them
☐ (i) only
☐ (ii) only
☐ Both (i) and (ii)

16.4 **Which of the following statements is/are correct?**

1. A company with only cash cows and dogs in its product portfolio has limited long term prospects.

2. A company with only question marks and dogs in its product portfolio will struggle to support and develop the former into stars and cash cows.

☐ Neither (1) nor (2)
☐ (1) only
☐ (2) only
☐ Both (1) and (2)

16.5 When operating in a new country, an organisation has to adapt its human resource management (HRM) policies and practices to suit local conditions.

Which of the following factors must be considered in relation to the organisation's HRM policies and practices?

Select all that apply.

☐ Local culture
☐ Exchange rates
☐ Interest rates
☐ Quality of local employees
☐ Adaptation of product to local market
☐ Appropriate management style

16.6 An IS/IT strategy must deal with three issues: the organisation's overall business needs; the organisation's current use of IT; and the potential opportunities and threats that IT can bring. Certain things should be done when developing an IS/IT strategy.

Which of the activities below deal with the organisation's overall business needs?

Select all that apply.

- ☐ Identify gaps in system coverage
- ☐ Encourage creative thinking
- ☐ Consider how IT can support business objectives
- ☐ Define business objectives
- ☐ Assess how good the current systems are, both technically and in terms of their value to the business

16.7 At a meeting to discuss the development of a new information system, Jane is putting forward the advantages of outsourcing.

Which of the following advantages would she include in her proposal?

Select all that apply.

- ☐ Long-term contracts allow much greater certainty in planning for the future
- ☐ An outsourcing company has economies of scale
- ☐ New skills and knowledge become available
- ☐ Outsourcing transfers system implementation to users
- ☐ Outsourcing allows increased management control

16.8 Triggers for change can either be internal or external.

Which of the following are internal triggers for change?

- ☐ Initiatives introduced by a new CEO who has just joined the organisation
- ☐ A new organisational structure which leads to new job responsibilities
- ☐ The implementation of a new IT system
- ☐ New laws or regulations affecting the industry
- ☐ Two competitors merging

16.9 Johnson, Scholes and Whittington identified five styles of change management.

Which one of these styles is based on persuasion?

- ☐ Education and communication
- ☐ Collaboration/participation
- ☐ Intervention
- ☐ Direction
- ☐ Coercion/edict

16.10 Kaplan and Norton (who developed the Balanced Scorecard) recommend that organisations implementing the Scorecard follow a four stage process for doing so.

What is the correct order of the process Kaplan and Norton recommend?

- ☐ Business planning; Translating the vision; Communicating and linking; Feedback and learning
- ☐ Translating the vision; Communicating and linking; Feedback and learning; Business Planning
- ☐ Business planning; Communicating and linking; Translating the vision; Feedback and learning
- ☐ Translating the vision; Communicating and linking; Business planning; Feedback and learning

17 Mixed Bank 5

17.1 X plc has traditionally developed its corporate strategy by analysing its markets and competitors to try to ensure that its strategic plans provide a good fit with its environment. However, the new CEO has argued that the increasingly dynamic nature of X's environment means that it is becoming increasingly difficult to predict the future with any certainly. Therefore, he has argued that X's strategy should focus more on its own capabilities.

How should X's traditional approach to strategic planning, and the approach now being suggested by the new CEO be classified?

Traditional approach:	☐ Accounting-led	☐ Position-based	☐ Resource-based
New CEO's approach:	☐ Accounting-led	☐ Position-based	☐ Resource-based

---

17.2 The arguments for and against social responsibility are complex.

The traditional approach to social responsibility is best summed up by which of the following?

☐ Organisations exist for the benefit of all stakeholders
☐ Organisations exist for the benefit of shareholders
☐ Organisations are social arrangements
☐ Organisations are political systems

17.3 **Which of the features below is the most important feature of good quality information?**

☐ Complete accuracy
☐ Absolute conciseness
☐ Relevance
☐ Rapidity of production

17.4 **Which of the following combinations of characteristics correctly defines a cash cow on the BCG matrix?**

☐ High market share, high industry growth rate
☐ High relative market share, high industry growth rate
☐ High market share, low industry growth rate
☐ High relative market share, low industry growth rate

17.5 **Which of the following statements are true**

(i) Franchising allows a business to expand using less capital than if it grows organically.

(ii) There is less scope for a company's reputation to be damaged if it grows by franchising than if it grows organically.

☐ Neither of them
☐ (i) only
☐ (ii) only
☐ Both of them

17.6 Two terms recur in the evaluation of any system – efficiency and effectiveness – and they are two key reasons for the introduction of information systems into an organisation.

Identify the THREE examples of efficiency from the following:

☐ Automation is pursued because the company expects it to help increase market share or satisfy customer needs.

☐ The speed of processing is improved.

☐ The cost of a computer system is lower than the manual system it replaces, mainly because the jobs previously performed by human operators are now done by computers.

☐ The accuracy of data/information and processing is improved, because a computer is less likely to make mistakes.

☐ Front office systems are developed to improve the organisation's decision-making capability.

17.7 **Which one of the following statements best represents 'a marketing orientation'?**

☐ Support for the marketing department from top management
☐ Ensuring a firm's product occupies a distinct place in the mind of target customers
☐ Creating demand for a firm's products
☐ A focus on supplying customer needs

17.8 **Which THREE of the following changes in the environment will improve sales for a brewery?**

☐ Reduction in the legal age for drinking
☐ Tightening of drink driving legislation
☐ Increase in average household disposable income
☐ Change in tastes from draught to bottled beers
☐ Increased emphasis on healthy living
☐ Tightening of border controls reducing illegal imports

17.9 **Which one of the following is NOT a potential disadvantage of bottom up change in an organisation?**

☐ It can be slower to implement than top down changes

☐ It can produce more unpredictable consequences than top down changes because it is subject to interpretation by the staff

☐ It may need to be imposed on an organisation in a crisis situation

☐ Senior management have less control over the change process

17.10 Shareholder value as a performance measure has increased in popularity because of concerns about the reliability of profit as a single measure of performance.

How is shareholder value calculated?

☐ Profit adjusted for long term investment on intangibles such as marketing, R&D and training
☐ NPV of future cash flows discounted at the cost of capital
☐ It is a subjective method of valuing a business to a shareholder
☐ Profit after accounting adjustments such as depreciation and bad debts

18 Mixed Bank 6

18.1 C plc intends to pursue a new corporate strategy geared around some new start-of-the-art plant and machinery.

Which aspect of Johnson, Scholes and Whittington's resources and competences is C relying upon?

- ☐ Strategic capability
- ☐ Tangible resources
- ☐ Threshold competences
- ☐ Intangible resources

18.2 When reading an article on stakeholders, Veronica is surprised at how many stakeholders there are and the different 'stakes' they have in the organisation. She is finding it difficult to distinguish between the various groups.

Which of the following would be described as connected stakeholders?

Select all that apply.

- ☐ Central government – interested in tax revenues and compliance with legislation
- ☐ Shareholders – want a return on their investment
- ☐ Suppliers – will expect to be paid and will be interested in the future
- ☐ Customers – want products and services
- ☐ Employees – want security of income and interesting work

18.3 PPI plc is exploring for oil in an area previously believed to have substantial, but difficult to extract reserves. Recent advances in hydraulic fracturing technologies ('fracking') mean that, as long as oil prices remain above certain levels, it may now be economical to move towards extraction.

Initial financial analysis indicates that PPI's investment in the technologies is likely to produce a negative NPV, unless shale gas is also discovered and can be extracted.

Which of the following techniques will allow PPI plc to factor in the financial impact of any potential shale gas reserves?

- ☐ Real options
- ☐ Delphi technique
- ☐ Scenario planning
- ☐ Regression analysis

18.4 Speedies Ltd manufactures a wide range of clothing and accessories for both amateur and professional swimmers. As part of a strategic review the senior management of the company have been asked to submit their thoughts its current strengths and weaknesses across a number of areas. A consensus was reached that the areas in which most improvement was required were:

(i)   Supplier relations
(ii) Quality of the management reporting pack

Which areas of the 9 M's model have been identified as weaknesses?

Select all that apply.

- ☐ Management Information Systems
- ☐ Make-up
- ☐ Markets
- ☐ Materials
- ☐ Methods

18.5 **Which of the following does NOT represent a drawback of globalisation?**

- ☐ Difficulties with co-ordinating activities
- ☐ Increased risk of focusing on a single market
- ☐ Potential relocation costs for key staff
- ☐ Lack of local knowledge

18.6 Bionic Buttons Ltd ('Bionic') is a company that manufactures computer peripherals such as keyboards and mouses. Historically, the company was successful due to a number of patented technological innovations. However, in more recent times competitors have developed equally effective, and at times, better products using alternative and emerging technologies. It has now been decided that, alongside continued investment in Research and Development, Bionic should also seek to develop much stronger customer relations, and better competitor intelligence. To this end the Director of IT has been commissioned to develop specialist in-house software to ensure that Bionic can build sustainable competitive advantage in these areas.

To date little progress has been made, owing to differences in opinion on how to proceed. The Director of IT believes that a top-down approach to developing a strategy would be best, as it would clearly relate to the new business objectives. This has been met with resistance from the more vocal members of his team who believe more emphasis should be placed on involving system users and internal specialists.

In terms of the three approaches that Earl identified in his 'three leg analysis' (business led; infrastructure led; and mixed) how should the views of the Director of IT and his team members be classified?

Director of IT:	☐ Business led	☐ Infrastructure led	☐ Mixed
Team members:	☐ Business led	☐ Infrastructure led	☐ Mixed

18.7 **Which one of the following is NOT a valid benefit or advantage of conducting customer profitability analysis?**

- ☐ It enables resources to be focused on the most profitable areas
- ☐ It identifies unexpected differences in profitability between customers
- ☐ It highlights the benefit of retaining existing customers
- ☐ It is a simple exercise

18.8 Bob is the Managing Director of a construction firm that has struggled in recent years. He has concluded that, in order to turn around its fortunes and be more successful in winning contracts, it needs to have a greater focus on quality. After discussions with other senior managers, Bob has decided that any change programme needs to be gradual, and that the outcomes will leave the firm operating within its existing paradigm.

According to Balogun and Hope Hailey's change matrix, what type of change is Bob describing?

- ☐ Adaptation
- ☐ Evolution
- ☐ Reconstruction
- ☐ Revolution

18.9 As well as top management commitment, establishing new norms that will assist in generating a new culture requires other actions.

Identify THREE of these actions from the list below:

- ☐ Support for positive behaviour and confrontation of negative behaviour
- ☐ Communication of desired norms
- ☐ New leadership to force the changes on people
- ☐ Recruitment and selection of the right people
- ☐ Getting rid of people that do not fit

18.10 Scary plc runs a large theme park in the north of England. The company is considering two different types of theme park attraction as possibilities for a future major investment. Both attractions involve an investment of approximately £1.5m.

Which of the following pieces of information will be LEAST significant for the decision?

☐ Prior years' customer data by type of attraction
☐ Demographic profile of the local population
☐ Competitor information on future new rides under construction
☐ Interest rate expectations for future borrowing

19 Mixed Bank 7

19.1 AZ Co is an electronics company based in a European country, and it uses a rational model approach to strategic planning. AZ is currently looking to expand aboard into other European countries. The European electronics market is known to be dynamic, and to contain a number of fast-moving, innovative companies

Two comments have been made about AZ Co's approach to strategic planning:

(i) Its approach to strategic planning will allow it to adapt quickly to deal with unexpected changes in the market.

(ii) Its approach to strategic planning will allow AZ to develop a picture of the opportunities and threats the European market presents before it decides to enter that market.

Which of the comments about AZ Co is/are true?

☐ Neither of them
☐ (i) only
☐ (ii) only
☐ Both (i) and (ii)

19.2 Objectives are seen as important within any organisation.

Which THREE of the following strategic activities are objectives useful for?

☐ To generate strategies for the company
☐ To write a mission statement
☐ To assess stakeholder power
☐ To determine operational priorities
☐ To control the company

19.3 Pepper Ltd follows a strategy which it thinks will be beneficial to it, but because of the response of its competitors the strategy turns out to be detrimental to both Pepper Ltd and the industry as a whole.

Which one of the following does this scenario relate to most closely?

☐ Emergent strategy
☐ Game theory
☐ Gap analysis
☐ Delphi technique

19.4 One of the criticisms of Porter's Value Chain is that the model is difficult to apply to service companies and network organisations. Stabell and Fjeldstad address these limitations by proposing new lists of primary activities in their Value Shop model.

Which THREE of the following are primary elements of Stabell and Fjeldstad's Value Shop model?

☐ Problem solving
☐ Responsiveness
☐ Choice between solutions
☐ Solution implementation
☐ Customer retention management

19.5 **Which of the following would be an example of product development for a carpet retailer operating a single store?**

☐ Opening a new carpet store in the next town
☐ Opening a new store in the next town, selling wooden flooring
☐ Selling wooden flooring in the existing store
☐ Increasing warehouse space to hold more carpets

19.6 Fruttie Fashions is a high street fashion chain that uses 'fast fashion' principles whereby it aims to offer at least 12 different clothing ranges each year, rather than the four seasonal collections which clothing retailers have traditionally offered. In order to constantly fill its shops with new designs, Fruttie Fashions relies heavily upon the ability of its designers to come up with attractive new lines; and upon fast and reliable communications with its overseas suppliers in order to be able to deliver orders on time. As a result, Fruttie Fashions invests heavily in its Enterprise Resource Planning (ERP) software and hardware infrastructure. Continual reinvestment in these systems is required to ensure the smooth logistics required to support the fast fashion sales model.

Using Peppard's Application Portfolio, how should the ERP system at Fruttie Fashion be classified?

☐ High potential
☐ Support
☐ Strategic
☐ Key operational

19.7 **Which one of the following best describes the difference between transaction marketing and relationship marketing?**

☐ Transaction marketing tracks customer payments
☐ Transaction marketing tracks the outstanding balances on credit customers' accounts
☐ Transaction marketing focuses on a single sales transaction at a time
☐ Transaction marketing focuses on customer benefits rather than product features

19.8 The Scottson Technology Institute (STI) is a government funded University, specialising in technology and science. The majority of its funding comes from a combination of the central government grants it receives, and the relatively modest tuition fees it is allowed to charge. Aside from this, income is generated by securing research grants and by encouraging private donations from STI alumni.

In recent years, STI has struggled to operate within its budgets as its government grants have been cut, donations have fallen, and research grants have been harder to secure. Whilst student demand continues to outstrip the supply of places available, a cap on fees has seen this income stream fall in real terms. The financial situation is becoming perilous and a new Vice Chancellor has been appointed to oversee the financial rescue of STI.

The new Vice Chancellor has therefore proposed a wage freeze for all staff for the next two years, whilst at the same time launching an aggressive fund-raising campaign aimed at significantly increasing the level of private donations from past students, targeting those who have not donated before. The Vice Chancellor has also joined a lobbying group with the aim of reversing the cut in government grants. The government has however recently promised not to allow tuition fees to rise for the next three years so as to encourage more students to pursue higher education.

STI's staff are angry at the proposed wage freeze and are being balloted for strike action.

Using Lewin's Force Field analysis, classify the following factors according to whether they are driving change or restraining it.

New Vice Chancellor	☐ Driving force	☐ Restraining force
Lobbying group	☐ Driving force	☐ Restraining force
Government policy	☐ Driving force	☐ Restraining force
Current private donors	☐ Driving force	☐ Restraining force
STI staff	☐ Driving force	☐ Restraining force

19.9 **Balogun and Hope Hailey analyse change by reference to its scope and its nature. According to their change matrix, what type of change is an incremental process which leads to a new paradigm?**

☐ Reconstruction
☐ Adaptation
☐ Evolution
☐ Transformation

19.10 **Which one of the following is NOT one of the three criteria a transfer pricing method should meet?**

☐ Commerciality
☐ Equity
☐ Neutrality
☐ Administrative simplicity

20 Mixed Bank 8

20.1 Mintzberg identified that in order for organisations to realise their intended strategies those strategies have to be 'crafted'.

Which of the following does Mintzberg refer to as essential activities in strategic management and crafting strategies?

Select all that apply.

☐ Managing instability
☐ Detecting continuity
☐ Know the business
☐ Manage patterns
☐ Reconcile change and continuity

20.2 An organisation should ensure that there is no conflict between its objectives, and that lower-level, more detailed objectives support the higher-level, more general ones.

What word is used to summarise this state of mutual support?

- ☐ Functionality
- ☐ Objectivity
- ☐ SMART
- ☐ Congruence

20.3 Forecasts, projections and regression analysis are three statistical techniques which managers can use to try to predict what is likely to happen in the future.

Identify which of the following descriptions relates to which technique (forecast; projection; regression analysis).

A quantitative technique to check any underlying correlations between two variables. ☐

An expected future trend pattern obtained by extrapolation. It is principally concerned with quantitative factors, rather than accounting for personal judgements. ☐

A prediction of future events and their quantification for planning purposes. ☐

20.4 Sarger Ltd is one of the 'Big Three' package holiday companies specialising in holidays for retired people in Country D. The company was formed 15 years ago and has steadily increased its market share over this period, during which the market as a whole has continued to grow at over 20%. Market growth is underpinned by a growth in both the number of retired people, and increases in their levels of disposable income.

Sarger's turnover in the last year was $78m, compared to $58m for 'Hols4U' and $98m for 'Retirement Breaks'.

The founder of Sarger Ltd has just retired himself and has sold the entire share capital to a national conglomerate Giga plc.

From the perspective of Giga plc, how would Sarger Ltd be classified using the Boston Consulting Matrix?

- ☐ Question mark
- ☐ Star
- ☐ Cash Cow
- ☐ Dog

20.5 A _____ is the purchase of a business from its existing owners by members of the current management team, generally in association with a financing institution.

What is the missing term?

- ☐ Demerger
- ☐ Management buy in
- ☐ Management buy out
- ☐ Retrenchment

20.6 **Match the descriptions of software applications (A – E below) to the systems which they describe**

(A) Processes large volumes of data via real time or batch processes

(B) Uses data and data analysis tools to support semi-structured choices

(C) Delivers high level outputs, using data from internal and external sources and using historic, current and future information

(D) Stores and integrates data from a range of operating systems across all business units

(E) Converts data from mainly internal sources into report formats

Management Information System (MIS) ☐

Decision Support System (DSS) ☐

Enterprise Resource Planning System (ERPS) ☐

Executive Information System (EIS) ☐

Transaction Processing System (TPS) ☐

20.7 **Which TWO of the following would be valid reasons for segmenting a market?**

☐ Demand for the product is greater than supply
☐ The level of competitiveness within the market is high
☐ The company has limited resources
☐ The product is totally unique and difficult to copy

20.8 Baloo Industries Ltd was acquired last year by Mowgli plc. The integration did not go as planned due to unforeseen difficulties integrating software and differences in corporate cultures of the companies. A decision therefore was taken to implement Mowgli's software and hardware infrastructure across the combined group. However, cultural integration remained problematic.

Following a review of the differing corporate cultures it was determined that significant differences would need to be resolved in the areas of symbols and structure.

Which model is being used to analyse corporate culture by Mowgli plc?

☐ McKinsey 7S model
☐ Cultural Web
☐ Hofestede's cultural dimensions
☐ Schein's model of organisational culture

20.9 **If management want to change the culture of an organisation, the least direct way of doing so will be to alter which of the following features?**

☐ Reward policies
☐ The organisation's product
☐ Staff selection
☐ Management style

20.10 **Which of the statements below are true of a policy of decentralisation and delegation?**

Select all that apply.

☐ Decisions are made at one point and so are easier to co-ordinate.
☐ There is greater awareness of local problems by decision makers.
☐ There is greater speed of decision-making and faster response to changing events.
☐ Policies, procedures and documentation can be standardised across the organisation.
☐ It is possibly cheaper, because fewer managers need be employed.

Answers to Objective Test questions

1 Fundamentals of strategic management

1.1   The correct answer is: Emergent.

The biggest clue is the fact that demand was unanticipated (in other words the move into selling material was in response to outside influence).

The key things to remember with emergent strategy are that strategy is not necessarily planned, and it does not necessarily come from ideas generated by people at the top of the organisation. It can be generated in response to suggestions or observations made by more junior staff members, or in response to outside influences.

1.2   The correct answers are:

- It focuses on the long term even if the market is extremely dynamic
- Generating strategy is a cultural and psychological process that cannot be forced
- It only allows ideas that have been generated through the formal process

The only options that do not correctly criticise the rational model are:

It focuses on objectives - the model **does** focus on objectives and

It focuses on resources - the model **does** take account of environmental factors via the environmental scanning phase.

The rational model is a formal process, that tends to work slowly, rigidly and to a formula.

1.3   The correct answer is: The system by which organisations are directed and controlled.

Corporate governance does not describe legal rules. It is the systems put in place by the directors to direct and control the organisation. This includes all members of staff, not just senior management.

1.4   The correct answer is: (3), (2), (1), (4), (5).

Objectives follow mission as they are based upon the latter. Corporate appraisal (SWOT analysis) follows the environmental analysis and position audit as it pulls the two together.

1.5   The correct answer is: Emergent strategy.

Emergent strategy 'emerges' from the activities and processes taking place at all levels of an organisation, in contrast to strategies that come from top-down, intended managerial processes.

The test of whether a strategy is realised or unrealised is whether what managers intended has actually been achieved (realised).

1.6   The correct answers are:

Opportunistic	**Informal**
Incremental	**Informal**
Rational model	**Formal**

The rational model provides a formal approach to strategy. Although a formal approach has a number of advantages (such as identifying the risks an organisation faces) it can also have problems (especially in fast-moving, dynamic environments).

Therefore, organisations have also used a range of less formal approaches to strategic planning in an attempt to address the problems inherent in the rational model. These informal approaches include: freewheeling opportunism, incrementalism, and emergent strategies.

1.7   The correct answer is: An operational strategy and a deliberate strategy.

Strategy can be categorised into corporate strategy (what business should we be in?), business unit strategy (how to approach a particular market or business unit) and operational strategy (decisions of strategic importance taken at operational level, such as investment in plant and investment in personnel). The strategy described here is a manufacturing strategy, ie an operational strategy.

Strategy can also be categorised into emergent and deliberate. An emergent strategy is one that develops without management's conscious intention, while a deliberate strategy arises from careful planning. The decision to bring in lean manufacturing techniques from the car industry is clearly a deliberate strategy rather than an emergent one.

1.8   The correct answer is: All commercial and not-for-profit bodies.

Whilst corporate governance is mostly discussed in relation to large publicly-quoted companies, it is an issue for all bodies corporate.

1.9   The correct answer is: Boards composed of relatively elderly directors.

The age of directors is not in itself a corporate governance issue.

1.10   The correct answer is: Exploit the organisation's distinctive competences.

A resource based approach identifies distinctive competences within the company and then exploits those strengths to create sustainable competitive advantage that is difficult to imitate.

However, this is not enough to guarantee success. Every company should also consider environmental factors, adjusting its strategies to the opportunities and threats that it perceives around it. This is the basis of position-based approaches to strategic planning.

2 Corporate objectives and stakeholders

2.1   The correct answer is: Customers have shifted from minimal effort to keep satisfied.

Historically customers were ignored, so would have been classified as 'Minimal effort' in Mendelow's matrix ie Low Power and Low Interest, given that individual customers exert little or no influence over strategy. The advent of social media has increased their power to 'high' given their ability to influence other potential customers through their comments, and the greater visibility of those comments. As such, being 'High Power' and 'Low Interest' means that customers have shifted to 'Keep Satisfied'.

2.2   The correct answer is: Integrity.

The FD is prepared to make a statement which contains dishonest information, knowingly failing to disclose the impending legal claim. This equates to a lack of integrity. Objectivity refers to work that is biased; confidentiality would relate to the unauthorised sharing of information. Professional competence would be attempting work without the necessary skills, and professional behaviour is concerned with personal insolvency and/or criminal behaviour.

2.3   The correct answers are:

*   Sustainability can help KPN reduce costs and improve efficiency
*   Sustainability can help KPN to comply with laws and regulations and to avoid fines
*   Sustainability can help protect KPN's reputation of KPN with stakeholders

The benefits of sustainability to KPN will include cost reductions and efficiency; compliance with laws and regulations (which reduces fines) and helping to protect the company's reputation. However, sustainability plans will not necessarily reduce the environmental impact as the production processes may not form part of a sustainability initiative. Similarly it is not necessary for KPN to take a lead in such matters. If it chooses to follow the sustainability strategies of its rivals it will not take the lead in shaping society.

2.4   The correct answers are:

- Level of interest.
- Level of power

Stakeholders with a low interest and low power require little consideration in objective setting, whereas key players, who have a high level of interest and power, must be considered during the planning process.

2.5   The correct answer is: Mito Care will be the global leader in cutting edge eye surgery.

Wishing to be the global leader is the only statement that focusses on the future desired state of the organisation eg where it wants to be. The other statements are more relevant to the mission statement, eg what the organisation does now, and how it does this.

2.6   The correct answer is: Stress to the government of JLR's home country the jobs that winning the contract could create and lobby them to ask the government of Country E to include JLR in the tender.

Given the tough laws on bribery in JLR's home country, the decision to appoint a minister from Country E is not advised as this may fall foul of the law. Undertaking a campaign in Country E is mis-directed as the population has little or no influence on the decision, and the same applies to the inoculation programme. The most sensible approach is for JLR to work with the government of its own country, as it may be able to communicate with Country E through established diplomatic channels.

2.7   The correct answers are:

Understanding of the key sustainability drivers of an organisation	**Strategy and oversight**
Extensive and effective sustainability training	**Execution and alignment**
Integration of the key sustainability drivers into the organisation's strategy	**Strategy and oversight**
Champions to promote sustainability and celebrate success	**Performance and reporting**

The full list of headings and elements as listed in CIMA's report is as follows:

Strategy and oversight:

- Board and senior management commitment (to sustainability)
- Understanding and analysing the key sustainability drivers for the organisation
- Integrating the key sustainability drivers into the organisation's strategy

Execution and alignment

- Ensuring that sustainability is the responsibility of everyone in the organisation (and not just of a specific department)
- Breaking down sustainability targets and objectives for the organisation as a whole into targets and objectives which are meaningful for individual subsidiaries, divisions and departments
- Processes that enable sustainability issues to be taken into account clearly and consistently in day-to-day decision-making
- Extensive and effective sustainability training

Performance and reporting

- Including sustainability targets and objectives in performance appraisal
- Champions to promote sustainability and celebrate success
- Monitoring and reporting sustainability performance

2.8   The correct answer is: Advocacy threat.

An advocacy threat occurs if a professional accountant is promoting a client or employer's position or opinion to the extent that the accountant's subsequent objectivity is compromised.

A self interest threat occurs if a financial or other interest inappropriately influences the accountant's judgment or behaviour.

A self review threat is the danger that the accountant will not properly evaluate the results of a previous judgment (by themselves or another member of their organisation) but they will then rely on that judgment as part of a current service they are providing.

An intimidation threat arises when the accountant is deterred from acting objectively by an actual or perceived threat.

2.9   The correct answers are:

- To provide good working conditions and decent rewards for all employees
- To keep employees informed of policy, progress and problems
- To support the local community and preserve the environment

By paying a minimum wage to everyone, and conforming with legislation, the organisation is fulfilling its legal obligations, not its social responsibilities.

2.10   The correct answer is: VERY POOR: He failed to identify the facts. No professional advice was sought and the issue remained unresolved.

Whilst it appears that the ACMA's actions are reasonable (in raising the matter with his manager), the actions taken are inadequate. The ACMA had only 'heard rumours' but didn't investigate further to identify whether they were true or not. The issue appears to remain unresolved (because the manager felt there was no need to investigate it further) making the 'Very Poor' description the correct assessment of the situation.

2.11   The correct answer is: Side payments

The primary objective of the local companies is to prevent the influx of foreign companies into the new economic zone. The government doesn't appear willing or able to meet this objective (by abandoning its plans to create the new zone) but instead it is trying to ensure that the local companies are compensated in another way (by meeting their demands for improved infrastructure).

Satisficing would involve negotiations between the key stakeholder groups to reach a compromise which is acceptable to them all. Sequential attention would involve focusing on the needs of different groups in turn, and on the understanding that once they have had their needs addressed they will then have to 'wait their turn' while the needs of other groups are addressed.

Exercise of power occurs if there is no other way of resolving conflicting views, so a senior figure forces through a decision by virtue of the power they possess.

2.12   The correct answer is: Philanthropic responsibility

Philanthropic responsibilities relate to behaviours and actions which are desired rather than being required by companies.

N Co does not appear to have any legal requirement to make the donation (legal responsibility), and the donation goes beyond the level of behaviour which would be expected of it ethically or morally (ethical responsibilities).

Economic responsibilities recognise that companies should act in a way which enables them to maintain a strong competitive position and to be as profitable and efficient as possible. While the donation could help improve N Co's reputation which could in turn help to boost sales and profits, the donation is not primarily designed to boost N's competitive position.

2.13   The correct answers are: CEO – Laissez-faire;   Marketing director – Enlightened self-interest

Organisations which adopt a laissez-faire stance take the view that an organisation's only responsibilities are the short-term interests of shareholders, and to make a profit, pay taxes and provide jobs.

The rationale behind the 'enlightened self-interest' stance (also known as 'long-term shareholder interest' stance) is that there can be a long-term benefit to shareholders from well-managed relationships with other stakeholders. Therefore, the justification for social action is that it makes good business sense. The organisation's corporate impact may be enhanced by assuming wide responsibilities; while exercising corporate power responsibly may prevent a social and political pressure for increased regulation of an organisation's activities.

A multiple stakeholder obligation recognises that organisations would not be able to function without appropriate relationships with stakeholder groups such as suppliers, employers and customers, so the expectations of these groups are equally important as those of its stakeholders.

The 'shaper of society' view is that financial performance is less important than the contribution an organisation makes to society as a whole.

2.14   The correct answer is: Trades unions; Non-governmental organisations; environmental groups

Civil society includes non-governmental organisations (NGOs), charities, trades unions, social and religious groups, environmental groups, professional associations, consumer groups, and the media.

Braithwaite and Drahos classify local residents with a common concern about an issue (such the new factory) as mass publics, rather than civil society.

Civil society is sometimes referred to as the 'third sector' on the basis that it is distinct from government and business.

3 The environment and uncertainty

3.1   The correct answers are:

- Increased competitive rivalry
- Market entry by new competitors
- Increased threat from substitutes

In a mature market, competitors will need to fight harder to gain (or even retain) sales, due to the lack of growth in the market. This will lead to increased rivalry amongst existing competitors. Combined with this, some late entrants will try and enter the market because the static, but high, volumes allow for large economies of scales using established technologies. Any mature market is subject to the risk of newer substitute products. These three forces will combine to put pressure on volumes and profits.

In a mature market, neither suppliers nor buyers are likely to exert higher pressure as both should be satisfied by high volumes and choice. This is supported by the statements on prices and costs in the question.

3.2   The correct answer is: Competitor analysis, Porter's five forces analysis, Industry life cycle analysis, PEST analysis.

Immediate profitability would be gained my mimicking successful competitor ploys. Longer terms gains would be made by, firstly, assessing the factors that constrain profitability (five forces), then understanding where the industry is headed (life cycle analysis) and finally by monitoring long term trends across the wider environment (PEST).

3.3 The correct answers are:

- They improve management's communication and awareness of complex issues affecting STI
- They provide some consensus amongst management on what STI should research in future
- They help STI's management to concentrate on the longer term despite the high uncertainty

Foresight has the benefits of improving communication and awareness of complex issues, providing consensus via techniques such as Delphi, and it helps retain a long-term focus during periods of high uncertainty. However, as foresight does not aim to forecast an exact vision of the future, it does not provide clarity over the future, nor does it facilitate any form of exact forecasting such as earnings from new projects.

3.4 The correct answer is: Prices will be high and demand will be relatively low.

The product life cycle indicates, that at the launch of any new technology, price skimming will be effective. This is because the company will need to recover the investment in R&D and cover the initially high unit production costs. Only the early adopters will purchase immediately (ie during the 'Introduction' phase of the life cycle) and they are happy to pay a premium to gain early access to the technology. Over time, as overall demand rises and economies of scale kick in, prices will begin to fall. However, during the initial launch phase, prices will remain high.

3.5 The correct answers are:

- Follow on investments should be factored into the initial investment decision
- Better information may become available to AAA if it delays its decision
- AAA should establish whether it is able to abandon the project part way through

Real options apply the Black-Scholes options pricing model to calculate the numeric value of having the options to:

1. follow on
2. delay
3. abandon

3.6 The correct answers are:

Force	Strength of force
Competitive rivalry	**Strong**
Bargaining power of customers	**Strong**
Threat of new entrants	**Weak**

The strong position of NW Bank and the well-established foreign banks suggest there will be a high level of rivalry in the banking market in Z Land.

The bargaining power of customers is likely to be high. There is little customer loyalty, and customers appear to have free choice over their banking arrangements.

The threat of new entrants is relatively weak. Although there are few structural barriers in place, the combination of a dominant player with governmental support, and the capital investment required to enter the market (B invested €600m to establish its branch network) make Z a relatively unattractive market to enter.

3.7 The correct answers are:

- The economic recession, leading to reduced funding
- Loss of staff to more secure charities

A threat is an external force, and as such the recession causing a fall in funding and the loss of staff to more secure charities. The lack of profile, and the reduced scope are both internal matters which would be classified as weaknesses. The merger with DD is harder to classify, as to whether it is an internal or external force. However, if it is classified as external, it should be seen as an opportunity for EE rather than a threat.

3.8   The correct answers are:

- A rise in interest rates.
- Devaluation of the euro.
- Increasing popularity of activity holidays.

A rise in interest rates would reduce discretionary spending as the cost of servicing existing loans, such as mortgages, becomes more expensive. Devaluation of the euro would mean that consumers will have to pay more for foreign currency and goods bought on overseas holidays would therefore become relatively more expensive. The increasing popularity of activity holidays would imply that consumer taste is moving away from cruise holidays.

As the airline industry does not compete with the cruise holiday industry, the change in technology should have little effect. The rise in the croupiers' wage rate and enhanced safety legislation may make cruises more expensive. Although this may later be passed onto holiday makers in the form of increased prices, which may then reduce demand, the impact is not a direct one.

3.9   The correct answers are:

Defining the scope of the project, and identifying major stakeholders	**1**
Developing quantitative models used to formulate competitive strategies	**5**
Developing learning scenarios and identifying further research needs	**4**
Identifying key trends and areas of uncertainty	**2**
Constructing initial scenarios and checking them for consistency	**3**

Shoemaker defined the stages in scenario planning as:

1. Defining the scope of the project, and identifying major stakeholders
2. Identification of key trends and areas of uncertainty
3. Constructing initial scenarios and checking them for consistency
4. Developing learning scenarios and identifying further research needs
5. Developing quantitative models used to formulate competitive strategies

3.10   The correct answers are:

- Time series
- Regression
- Delphi method

Environmental uncertainty forecasting techniques include time series, regression, econometrics, jury forecasts and the Delphi method. Visioning and Foresight are not forecasting techniques because rather than trying to create a single version of the future (ie a forecast) they attempt to create a range of possible outcomes from which contingent strategies can be derived.

4 Resources and capabilities

4.1   The correct answers are:

- Human resource management
- Service
- Marketing and sales

The problems within XPO lie within poorly trained sales staff and lack of skilled engineers (human resource management), the consequent mis-selling of systems (sales and marketing) and the resultant poor levels of customer service (service). There is no suggestion that the systems themselves are poorly built (operations) or are backed-up by inadequate systems (Technology development).

4.2   The correct answer is: Downstream supply chain management.

The upstream supply chain would refer to the suppliers of watch components, and the downstream supply chain would relate to customers and distributors. In this instance, the change is being driven by BB itself, hence there is no' upstream' aspect. The term 'value chain management' is too general to be correct, and there is no indication that BB is looking to develop a closer relationship with the retailer (its customer) as would be the case in customer relationship management.

Hence the correct answer is downstream supply chain management ie aligning the supply chain in a way that better serves customers, in this case the ultimate (end user) consumer.

4.3   The correct answer is: Mature products may not repay the opportunity cost of additional investment in them due to low margins and the danger of decline.

The BCG classifies products on the basis of relative market share (own share/share of strongest rival) being either High >1 or Low < 1, and market growth being either High >10% or Low < 10%. Products can be classified as follows:

High relative market share, High market growth – Star

High relative market share, Low market growth – Cash cow

Low relative market share, High market growth – Question mark

Low relative market share, Low market growth – Dog

In FDJ's case, because its market share is 60% (more than half of the market) it must have a relative market share of >1. Market growth (4%) is relatively low, however, making FDJ a Cash Cow. A suitable strategy for a Cash Cow will be determined by its ability to generate returns in excess of the cost of capital, in order to justify continuing investment in it. It is not true to say that FDJ has a low market share, will see its cash flows increase, or is selling a new product in a high growth market, making all of these options incorrect.

4.4   The correct answer is: Functional benchmarking

Functional benchmarking (which is sometimes also called operational benchmarking, or generic benchmarking) involves comparing the performance of internal functions with that of the best external practitioners, regardless of their industry.

If DEF was comparing its performance to other banks it would be undertaking competitive benchmarking, but it is comparing its performance with companies in very different industries, which means it is undertaking functional benchmarking.

4.5   The correct answer is: Question mark.

The market growth rate is high, but, as the product is being introduced by a small player in the market, its relative market share will be low. These factors combined mean the product is a Question mark.

4.6   The correct answers are:

- Effective rate of tax to sales ratio
- Company's cost of capital to sales ratio
- Operating profit to sales ratio

Rappaport identified seven drivers of value: Sales growth, Profit margins, Tax rates, Fixed asset investment, Length of projects, Working capital investment and Cost of capital. (These drivers can be remembered via the mnemonic Stupid People Take Far Longer With Crosswords).

P/E ratios and dividends fall outside the scope of the SVA model.

4.7   The correct answers are:

Identify how additional value can be generated by each activity performed | 4

Evaluate the requirements of BPM's customers | 2

Re-engineer activities where additional value can be added, consider reducing those that do not add significant value | 5

Create a multi-disciplinary project team | 1

Identify which activities add value to customers and categories them with the Value Chain | 3

This project should start with the assembly of a suitably skilled and experienced team. The team will then define what customers want in order to deduce the value that BPM should look to add. From here the relevant activities within BPM can be identified, and an assessment of how additional value can be generated undertaken. Finally activities can be re-engineered, and those not required can be reduced in importance, or even removed.

4.8   The correct answer is: Frequently changing suppliers.

Supply chain management involves working together with other companies to deliver goods and services to customers. It tends to encourage long-term relationships, rather than frequent changes in suppliers.

4.9   The correct answers are:

- The product is affected by environmental issues outside the control of the company
- The product is affected by internal decisions about the level of resources given to the product

The options that the product has a finite life-span, and passes through distinct phases describe the product life-cycle, and are thus not criticisms of the model.

4.10   The correct answer is: Selling.

Selling comes under the heading of marketing and sales.

5 Developing and evaluating strategic options

5.1   The correct answer is: A foreign direct investment strategy.

The acquisition of the foreign company is an example of foreign direct investment: 'a direct investment into production or business in a country by an individual or company of another country, either by buying a company in the target country or by expanding operations of an existing business in that country.'

Franchising would have involved working with franchisees to share the capital costs of expansion.

A transnational business conducts operations in several countries with varying degrees of coordination and integration of strategy and operations. However, as the chain it has acquired is only small, it seems unlikely that DD's head office, and control of the business, will move away from its existing base in country F.

An export strategy would have involved shipping domestic goods overseas for sale.

5.2   The correct answers are:

- QS will gain barriers to entry in its niche segment
- QS will need to reduce its product range
- QS will be more exposed to risk from a decline in this segment

The move to cost leadership will act as a barrier to entry, making it harder for other low cost producers to enter the market. In order to lower unit costs the product range will need to be reduced; otherwise the necessary economies of scale are unlikely to result. By choosing to focus on a single market segment QS will clearly be exposed to the risk that this segment will decline, reducing sales and undermining the cost savings achieved through economies of scale.

5.3   The correct answer is: (1) only.

Growth to global scale will inevitably lead to consideration of structure and probably bring pressure for a move to a decentralised form. This is because of the difficulty of centralising control of a large and disparate organisation operating under a variety of cultural, economic and legal influences and probably using more than one language.

When setting up a new operation overseas, several options are possible, including: a joint venture, use of an agent, an acquisition and the opening of a branch office. There are many factors to consider and one of these options should be chosen according to circumstances.

5.4   The correct answer is: Price skimming.

Price skimming sets an initially high price. This restricts sales volume but can produce good returns quickly. It is only feasible when the new product is sufficiently differentiated that competition is significantly restricted. Cost plus pricing might seem like an attractive option, but its drawback is that it ignores market conditions and so may lead to a price that is too high or low to maximise revenue in the early stages of the product life cycle.

5.5   The correct answer is: (i), (ii) & (iii)

A major disadvantage of joint ventures is that there can be conflicts of interest between the venture partners. These may arise over profit shares, amounts invested, management of the joint venture, or marketing strategy.

Profits from the venture have to be shared among the partners, reducing the amount each earns.

Partners can gain confidential information about each other, which one partner could subsequently use competitively against another.

5.6   The correct answer is: POOR: Evaluation is based on a flawed assessment of core competences and incorrect applications of Ansoff's Matrix and SAF analysis.

The CGMA has incorrectly used Ansoff's matrix as this is an example of Product, not Market, Development. The CGMA has also applied the SAF model incorrectly, because having the necessary competencies would fall under the 'Feasible' rather than the 'Suitable' category. Finally the concept of competency has been misunderstood as generating power from renewable sources will require very different competencies to using coal. However, assessing the CGMA's response as 'unacceptable' is incorrect, as the CGMA has shown some awareness of the concepts, even if they have not been applied correctly.

5.7   The correct answer is: 14.8%.

Current present value

Year		Cash flow $000	Discount factor	Discounted cash flows $000
0	Investment	(10,000)	1.000	(10,000)
1-3	Receipts	9,000	2.723	24,507
1-3	Costs	(4,000)	2.723	(10,892)
				3,615

Therefore sales must reduce by 3,615/24,507 = 14.8%.

Alternative working

Discounted sales receipts 24,507 - 3,615 = $20,892

Annual sales receipts = 20,892/2.723 = $7,672

Reduction in sales receipts = 9,000 − 7,672/9,000 = 14.8%.

5.8   The correct answer is: Taller vertical organisation structures.

As an organisation becomes more global, particularly through the use of the Internet, then the organisation structure tends to flatten. Power in global firms tends to be diffused to local operations.

5.9 The correct answers are:

Can generate multiple strategic options	**Benefit**
Requires interpretation to make it fit the circumstances of the organisation	**Drawback**
Not sufficient on its own to determine strategy	**Drawback**
Simple visual presentation of complex ideas	**Benefit**
Does not include means of achieving growth	**Drawback**
Long established and familiar to management	**Benefit**

Lynch's Matrix looks at the options for growth via the combination of decisions to drive growth internally or externally, and whether to expand domestically or overseas.

The benefits of the matrix include that it clearly shows multiple options, and in a simple graphical form. It is also an established model well understood by many managers.

The limitations of the matrix include criticisms that some interpretation is required to fit the circumstances, for instance it is possible for larger organisations to pursue multiple strategies at the same time – such as growing internally in some markets whilst franchising in others. Furthermore, the matrix does not provide any practical advice about how to implement the options to achieve growth. Finally, it is insufficient on its own to determine strategy, as other models such as Porter's generic strategies, value chain and Ansoff's matrix should also be deployed.

5.10 The correct answers are:

Purchase another woman's uniform manufacturer whose sole business is supplying the armed forces in UNS's home country	**Market Penetration**
Purchase a men's uniform manufacturer, based in another country, whose sole business is supplying the armed forces in UNS's home country	**Product Development**
Tender for that contracts to supply women's uniforms to the armed forces of another country	**Market Development**
Purchase a men's uniform manufacturer, based in another country, that has contracts with the armed forces of several countries	**Diversification**

This question refers to Ansoff's matrix which looks at the combination of markets and products:

Existing products and markets – market penetration
New products and existing markets – product development
Existing products and new markets – market development
New products and markets – diversification (related or unrelated)

6 Creating an IT strategy

6.1 The correct answer is: Mash-up.

A mash-up, in web development, is a web page, or web application, that uses content from more than one source to create a single new service displayed in a single graphical interface. For example, you could combine the addresses and photographs of your library branches with a Google map to create a map mash-up. In this case, potential lettings are combined with information on local businesses and local government websites.

Competence syndication involves the sharing of unique competences between businesses, but there is no indication that X is making use of competences offered by other businesses, nor sharing its competences with any other businesses.

X's website does more than share information, and is not a social media site as it does not encourage interaction between those that log on to the site.

6.2   The correct answer is: Viral advertising.

DTI's website has a social media aspect via the user uploads. Providing links to external sites such as accommodation and transport is indicative of mash-ups. The syndication of external data (such as news feeds) indicates competence syndication is taking place. There is no evidence of any viral advertising (marketing techniques that use pre-existing social networking services and other technologies to try to produce increases in brand awareness or to achieve other marketing objectives through self-replicating viral processes such as shared videos).

6.3   The correct answer is: Information technology (IT) strategy.

If you view these strategies as a hierarchy within an organisation you can see that the business strategy is developed first; from this the information systems strategy will set out what information requirements there are to enable the business plan to be met. From this the IT strategy and IM strategy are developed, the former relating to the choice of hardware and software, the latter being how the information should be managed.

6.4   The correct answers are:

- Queue lengths at tills
- Number of customer complaints
- Customer satisfaction scores

Number of returns is likely to be a performance indicator for the CSF of offering the correct quality and range of products (because it is a measure which can be used to assess whether the CSF is being achieved or not). Employee satisfaction scores will be a performance indicator for the CSF of having a happy and motivated workforce.

6.5   The correct answers are:

- External and internal information
- Both qualitative and quantitative information

A decision support system uses tactical information, which is derived from both external and internal sources, and is both qualitative and quantitative.

Information sources that are much more detailed and that cover a shorter time frame are used by lower management to make routine operational decisions. Strategic information tends to be long term and is externally focused.

6.6   The correct answers are:

- It is a potential source of competitive advantage for Catseye that should be managed strategically as well as operationally

- Changes in information strategy can have significant impacts on internal and external stakeholders that need to be handled strategically

- Expenditure on information systems is significant and often requires evaluation against both strategic initiatives and business operations

Michael Earl identified nine reasons why organisations should employ IT professionals at executive level, and why organisations need a strategic approach to IS/IT. The correct answers describe three of these nine reasons:

- Source of competitive advantage
- Impact on many stakeholders inside and outside an organisation
- Involves significant expenditure (high costs)

The points on careers and duplication were not addressed by Earl.

6.7 The correct answers are:

- Planning and controlling IS developments
- Allocating human resources within the IT department

The information management (IM) strategy defines the organisation's basic approach to the management of its information systems. The activities that fall within IM strategy are: planning and controlling IS developments, and the allocation of human resources within the IT department.

6.8 The correct answer is: Clear prioritisation of development projects and efficient use of the resources available.

The information management strategy focuses on the management of IT; if such a strategy is in place you would expect clear prioritisation of development projects and efficient use of the resources available.

The information technology strategy should deal with the minimum standards for software and hardware.

The information systems strategy should ensure that management reviews recent innovations with a view to assessing the relevance of those innovations to their business. The business should drive the process, rather than the technology driving it.

6.9 The correct answers are:

- IS and IT affect some levels of management
- IS and IT may need effective management to obtain maximum benefit from them

As IT and IS strategies affect the processes and information used by management it is likely that the IS/IT strategy would affect **all** levels of management rather than just some of them. Also, effective management will definitely be required if an organisation is to get the best from its IS/IT. The other justifications given are all relevant.

6.10 The correct answer is: An expert system must be designed from scratch.

An expert system does not need to be designed from scratch, as it is possible to buy off the shelf a shell system to which the required knowledge or expertise can be added. Expert systems are often heuristic, in that the rules are arrived at by trial and error, in a learning process, rather than by the operation of an algorithm.

6.11 The correct answer is: The industry that the company is in.

Having the right product mix available in each store, and having products available on the shelves for customers to buy at any time are prerequisites for an organisation's success in the supermarket industry as a whole, regardless of the detailed strategy a company is pursuing or its position in the industry.

The CSF has not been influenced by any external factors (eg PEST factors), or any unusual or temporary factors. An example of how temporal factors as a source of CSFs might be: if one of the supermarkets had recently been fined for selling out of date products, and so it added a CSF identifying the need for all products on the shelves to be within their sell by date.

7 Using IT strategically

7.1 The correct answers are:

- Webcasts
- Social media

BBL could use Webcasts to deliver online training, and Social Media such as Facebook pages and Twitter feeds to promote its business. CRM would help build long-term relationships and Powerpoint could be used as a training tool, but in itself neither is an example of Web 2.0 technology which would facilitate interaction and user-driven content.

7.2   The correct answers are:

Identify the Critical Success Factors of the strategy | 3

Set the targets for the organisation and its managers | 5

Set the strategic objectives of the organisation | 2

Establish mission of the organisation | 1

Establish the Key Performance Indicators | 4

A logical start point is the mission, as this creates a framework within which to work. Following the mission, which can be a little vague some specific 'SMART' objectives should follow. The CSFs that support the mission and objectives can then be identified ensuring the business understand what it needs to measure. To track performance in CSFs suitable KPIs can be defined allowing targets to be set.

7.3   The correct answer is: Basic e-commerce

SRB allows customers to place orders and pay for them online, and so it has moved beyond simply having a web presence (which is the first stage in the introduction of e-business).

However, the fact that SRB does not gather information about customers' purchasing habits indicates that it has not yet reached the integrated e-commerce stage (which is the third stage in the introduction of e-business). At the integrated e-commerce stage, organisations use electronic technology to develop closer relationships with their customers and suppliers.

Basic e-commerce (the second stage) is characterised by an organisation having the ability to deal directly with customer and suppliers, but not having made any significant changes to its underlying business model or processes.

7.4   The correct answer is: Upgrading the nominal ledger to the most recent version of the package.

This is unlikely to improve the quality of the information to such an extent that it will differentiate the organisation from the rest of the market. So, it will not confer competitive advantage.

If the quality of the decision-making improves significantly through the introduction of an expert system, the organisation will be better placed than its rivals. As such, it has gained a competitive advantage.

Being the first organisation to integrate the supply chain through the use of electronic data interchange is likely to produce competitive advantage because significant cost savings could be made.

If the senior management has access to better information through an executive information system, they are more likely to make better decisions. This has potential for creating competitive advantage (in the same way that an expert system has the potential to create competitive advantage).

7.5   The correct answer is: Data integrity and the elimination of duplication.

A single, central pool of data reduces the likelihood of inconsistencies – although this means that control over data is centralised rather than resting with end-users.

7.6   The correct answers are:

Knowledge Management Requirement		Organisational Tool
Creation of knowledge	A	Creation of sharing culture
Capture of knowledge	B	Database structure
Storage of knowledge	E	Technological infrastructure
Availability (dissemination) of knowledge	D	Intranet & Extranet
Utilisation of knowledge	C	Staff development and training

Creation of knowledge comes from sharing knowledge amongst staff. This is reliant upon culture. Capturing knowledge relies upon hardware and software such as databases. Storing knowledge requires a secure and reliable infrastructure. Making knowledge available can be done via networks linked to intranets and extranets. Once knowledge is captured in a usable format it can be exploited by providing training and development courses.

7.7   The correct answers are:

- Big data is the storing of organisational data in digital form

- Big data is the creation and analysis of a large internal data warehouse used to store all of an organisation's data relating to customers, staff, operations and products

The term 'Big data' is used to describe a massive volume of both structured and unstructured data that is so large that it's difficult to process using traditional database and software techniques. In most enterprise scenarios, the data is too big or it moves too fast or it exceeds current processing capacity. Big data has the potential to help companies improve operations and make faster, more intelligent decisions. These may include better understanding customer segments and perhaps using this understanding to improve product development.

Storing data in digital form refers to the process of 'digitisation' and although it will require the creation of data warehouses these refer to the architecture needed for analytics, not the big data itself.

7.8   The correct answer is: The service level agreement.

This contains vital information concerning the provision of the outsourcing service agreed by both parties.

7.9   The correct answer is: Increased user participation.

Web 2.0 allows internet users (and potential customers for businesses) to be no longer simply recipients of information, but to participate in the creation, sharing and evaluation of content. In other words, users can actively take part in 'many-to-many' communications. A crucial aspect of Web 2.0 is that it focuses on user experience and participation.

7.10   The correct answers are:

- Only employees are able to access information on an extranet   **False**
- Intronets allow suppliers and customers to gain privileged access to data held by the host   **True**

An extranet is a computer network that allows controlled access from outside of an organisation's intranet. Extranets are used for specific use cases including business-to-business (B2B).

When access to an extranet is extended to trusted external agencies, such as suppliers and customers, it becomes an intronet.

7.11   The correct answer is: The process of aligning and developing the capacities of a team to create the results its member truly desire.

That is the definition which Peter Senge (who developed the idea of learning organisations) gives for team learning.

The remaining options refer to some of the other characteristics which Senge identifies in learning organisations:

The recognition that organisations learn only through individuals who learn relates to the characteristic of 'personal mastery'. Although individual learning does not guarantee organisational learning, organisational learning cannot occur without individual learning; therefore all employees are encouraged to continually develop themselves.

The capacity to hold a shared picture of the future that an organisation seeks to create relates to 'shared vision'.

The ingrained assumptions and generalisations which influence how people understand the world and how they take action relates to 'mental models'.

8 Strategic marketing

8.1   The correct answer is: Computer-aided design.

The low volumes of the business make an automated warehouse unnecessary; similarly the need for e-procurement is also ruled out. In-store checkouts would be contrary to the high level of personal service the company offers to its exclusive clientele, leaving computer-aided design as the best investment. This system would speed up shoe construction, reduce human error, and improve the customer experience though faster delivery of better quality shoes.

8.2   The correct answers are:

- People
- Processes
- Physical evidence

The four Ps of the traditional marketing mix are:

- Product
- Place
- Price
- Promotion

When a service is being considered, the three additional Ps are added to make the seven Ps.

8.3   The correct answers are:

- The internal company sales database.
- Information received from market research agencies on sector sales.
- Competitor sales activity analysis.

The company's own sales database can be indicative of a trend that might mirror the general market and is therefore a useful source of information in that respect. Information from a market research agency can also be useful, although the incidence of bias can reduce the value. Competitor sales activity analysis is useful for spotting market trends and can be used to identify whether a company's own sales are indicative or are going against the trend.

Government demographic forecasts may be useful, but not in every sector.

Customer satisfaction surveys, although useful, will not necessarily provide any information about market trends. They will reveal what customers like, or don't like, about a company and its products or services, but not what products or services have sold well, or will sell well.

8.4   The correct answers are:

- The internet promotes transparent pricing   **True**
- E-marketing is primarily useful for customer retention rather than customer acquisition   **False**

The freely available information on the internet has increased the visibility and comparability of prices (price transparency).

E-marketing is used both to attract new customers and also to keep contact with existing customers via techniques such as email and SMS discount codes and marketing messages.

8.5   The correct answer is: Recommendations.

Search engines, comparison sites and affiliate marketing are all methods for acquiring customers.

However, recommendations are most useful for customer extension. For example, when an existing customer logs back into an online store, the customer is given recommendations for other products they might like to buy, based on their previous purchasing history.

8.6   The correct answer is: It ensures that the company is pursuing effective policies to promote its products and services.

The strategic component of marketing planning focuses on the direction which an organisation will take in relation to a specific market, or set of markets, in order to achieve a specified set of objectives.

Marketing-oriented companies segment their markets according to customers' differences (not by product), and tailor their marketing strategies according to different customer needs.

8.7   The correct answer is: (i) & (ii) only.

Relationship marketing devotes marketing resources to maintaining and exploiting an organisation's existing customer base, and it focuses on establishing loyalty among customers. As such, it focuses on customer retention and building customer loyalty.

However, it also encourages high customer contact, with each contact being used to improve information about the customer and build the relationship with the customer. By contrast, transactions marketing only encourages low or moderate contact with customers.

8.8   The correct answer is: Allocation of fixed overheads.

Fixed overheads will not change if the company's sales ledger grows or shrinks by one customer and should not therefore be included. The remaining options can be linked specifically to individual customers.

8.9   The correct answer is: Commitment to remaining competitive above all.

The other options are all characteristics of relationship marketing.

8.10   The correct answer is: Marketing mix.

The traditional marketing mix includes four variables (4 Ps): product, price, place and promotion but for services, the marketing mix is extended to include 7 Ps: product, price, place, promotion, people, processes and physical evidence.

8.11   The correct answer is: Influence markets.

Influence markets are made up of people or groups which can influence customer purchases, such as analysts, pressure groups or consumer groups. The need for an effective PR department is particularly important to ensure that a company if presented favourably to this market.

The analysts are not responsible for introducing new investors to X (as would be the case in a referral market) nor are they buyers of the shares themselves (customer market).

Recruitment markets relate to staff recruitment.

9 Organisational change

9.1 The correct answers are:

- The Board of XP encourages collaboration and partnerships with other organisations.
- XP's management has always been highly innovative in the services it provides.

According to Kanter, organisations which are change adept have the following characteristics:

- The imagination to innovate
- The professionalism to perform
- The openness to collaborate

Responding to competitors, analysing the environment, and developing a sophisticated website do not fall within with definition.

9.2 The correct answers are:

Current planning application process in Country H	**Restraining Force**
Z's customers	**Driving Force**
New managing director	**Driving Force**
Proposed planning laws	**Driving Force**
Local residents	**Restraining Force**

The changes are being driven by the new MD's desire for solar farms, the changing attitudes of customers towards renewable energy and the Government's proposed changes to the planning laws. Opposing change are the current process (which requires local consultation, and thereby enables local residents to obstruct the process) and the local residents themselves.

9.3 The correct answers are:

- Shared values
- Strategy
- Staff

The McKinsey 7 S model identifies three 'hard elements' of culture being Structure, Systems and Strategy. The four 'soft' elements are Style, Skills, Share Values and Staff. Stories and symbols are part of Balogun & Hope Hailey's Cultural web, rather than the McKinsey 7 S model. Software is not an element of culture.

9.4 The correct answer is: Change.

The unfreezing stage in Lewin's stage model of change is concerned mainly with selling the change and giving individuals a motive for changing their attitudes, values or systems. Refreezing is the final stage in Lewin's model, implying consolidation or reinforcement of new behaviour.

Culture change is not one of the stages of Lewin's model. However, it can be very difficult to change the culture of an organisation and doing so can often require alterations to the power structure within the organisation.

9.5 The correct answer is: Get team leaders to instruct others on the benefits of the change.

People who instruct others on a new viewpoint usually change their own ideas faster than those who just listen. Getting the team leaders on your side will improve the chances of the team loyalty shifting in favour of the change.

Paying the employees to change could ensure compliance with the change in the short term, however, it is very unlikely to change the employees' attitude, and there is the risk that it could be seen as bribery. This would further reduce respect for the change.

The presentation of the change as a 'done deal' may strengthen resistance due to resentment over the lack of information and consultation.

Lying to your staff is never a good idea. It is probable that they will find out the truth, when they do, this will create both more resentment and a lack of respect for you as their manager.

9.6   The correct answer is: Appoint a Change Agent to develop KYJ.

KYJ's management and staff appear to lack the experience needed to successfully drive change, however they are loyal, well-qualified and keen to be involved. The best approach therefore is to appoint a suitably experienced external change agent to help KYJ's staff to develop the solutions required.

9.7   The correct answer is: Revolution.

Balogun and Hope Hailey would identify the nature of the change as 'Big Bang' as Pear has launched a completely new product in a short period of time. The scope of change is 'transformational' because Pear's new product is completely different to its previous book products.

Changes which are 'Big Bang' in nature and transformational in scope as classified as Revolutionary in Balogun and Hope Hailey's matrix of change types. Revolutionary changes – fast-paced and wide-ranging – may often be needed to ensure an organisation's survival in response to extreme environmental changes.

9.8   The correct answers are:

- Changes in economic conditions such as the onset of a recession
- Changes in customer tastes and expectations
- A new competitor entering the market

External triggers come from the external environment outside an organisation. PEST analysis and Porter's five forces can often be useful models for identifying external factors for change.

Although the CEO has joined the organisation from outside he or she will then be employed by the organisation. So any new initiatives the CEO introduces which act as triggers for change come from the CEO working within the organisation, and are therefore internal.

Similarly, the decision to relocate a business unit is made within the organisation itself.

9.9   The correct answer is: (ii) only.

Theory O changes are concerned with developing an organisation's human capability to implement strategy. A key element of Theory O is that change is participative and emergent rather than being top-down and planned. Encouraging the staff to make suggestions and share ideas (as in Option ii) suggests a participative and emergent approach to change.

By contrast, in Theory E, change is viewed as a top-down process, and changes are planned and programmatic, and they focus on formal structure and systems.

Therefore, option (i) is more characteristic of a Theory E approach than a Theory O approach.

9.10   The correct answer is: The combined entities are worth more together than apart.

Synergies are sometimes described as being the '2 + 2 = 5' effect. Merged organisations can benefit from cost synergies (for example, headcount reduction; increased purchasing power and economies of scale; elimination of surplus facilities) or revenue synergies (for example, marketing and selling complementary products or services; or cross-selling into a new customer base or distribution channel). Synergies can also be gained from sharing knowledge and management skills.

As such, the other three options could all contribute to the synergies resulting from an acquisition or merger, but the fact that the combined entities are worth more together than apart provides the best overall description of synergy.

10 Leading and managing change

10.1   The correct answers are:

- Explicit and implicit coercion: policies of forced economies, redundancies and closures to reduce costs, and the introduction of changes to working practices.

- Negotiation and agreement: urgent meetings with trade union representatives to develop a plan to make PPI profitable and to incentivise employees by offering them a share in the profits of PPI when it is sold.

- Facilitation and support: announcement of generous financial packages and help with finding new jobs for staff who are willing to volunteer for redundancy from PPI, and provision of training to those staff willing to change job roles.

The high degree of antipathy amongst staff, coupled with the possibility of increased resistance via the trade union means that education and communication has already failed, and hence collaboration (participation and involvement) is unlikely to succeed either. The other options are all viable in the circumstances described.

10.2   The correct answers are:

- Setting a direction for the organisation
- Aligning people by communicating the direction of the strategy
- Motivating and inspiring staff to pursue the organisation's vision

Planning, budgeting, control and problem-solving are all part of 'business as usual' tasks for a CFO, and hence will not help with change leadership.

10.3   The correct answers are:

- Beliefs and values
- Customs
- Symbols

An example of a belief is 'the customer prefers good quality to cheaper prices'. Customs are acceptable ways of behaviour, which are sometimes enforced by rules, such as dress codes. Symbols or signs include company logos. Although ownership and technology are not included in the definition of organisational culture, there are companies whose owners determine the culture of the company and there are also companies that emphasise their involvement in new technology.

10.4   The correct answers are:

- Vision is poorly communicated
- Systems, policies and skills are not aligned
- Change is not perceived as urgent

Each of these factors are ones which Kotter identified as reasons why change initiatives could fail.

Having a clear vision for the change; creating short-term wins; and forming a guiding coalition with enough power to lead the change effort all support, rather than hinder, change.

10.5   The correct answer is: Intervention.

Intervention is undertaken by a change agent who delegates some aspects of the change process to teams or individuals, while providing guidance and retaining overall control.

10.6   The correct answer is: Inspirational

In an inspirational leadership style, leaders focus on developing meaningful visions for the future, through focusing on radically new ideas. Leaders learn by experimentation; they are inquisitive and curious, and satisfy their curiosity by finding radically new solutions.

The commanding style focuses on performance, and has a short-term goal orientation. The logical style pertains to leaders who insist on covering all alternatives. Supportive leaders emphasise openness and operate more as facilitators than directors. They learn by observing outcomes and how others react to their decisions.

10.7   The correct answer is:

- Participation and involvement: the trigger for change has not come from P, but the implementation of the change will benefit from the active participation and involvement of P and the IT staff.

If P and the IT staff feel they are involved in selecting the package required to replace CC's existing CRMS then they will be less likely to resist it.

Communication and education are not required, because P is already aware 0of the limitations of the existing CRMS.

Facilitation and support is not appropriate as there is no indication that the decision to introduce the new package represents a threat to P's role. The IT department may need support to overcome any disruption involved in migrating CC's marketing information to the new package, but question option refers specifically to P, rather than the department as a whole.

Manipulation and co-option is not needed because, although P is opposed to the change, it would be wrong to offer rewards to a director merely to carry out their job ie implementing new technologies which improve the competitive performance of their organisation.

10.8   The correct answer is: Someone who must adapt to the change.

Change recipients are those who must adopt change or adapt to it.

10.9   The correct answer is: Both of them.

Both of these are advantages of using an external change agent.

The external change agent can bring in experience and expertise which PHL doesn't have internally.

And the agent can recommend 'best practice' approaches, drawing on their experience from working with other organisations and on similar projects.

10.10   The correct answer is: Staff

The six manifestations of culture are: Stories; Symbols; Power structures; Organisational structures; Control systems; and Rituals and routines. Together these make up the paradigm, which signifies the underlying assumptions and beliefs which an organisation's decision-makers hold and take for granted.

10.11   The correct answers are:

- Successful companies encourage constant innovation
- Companies need the flexibility to be able to respond quickly to changes in the environment

Peters' notion of firms 'thriving on chaos' is based on the idea that the volatility and dynamism of the external environment means that companies need to the flexibility and responsiveness to be able to react quickly to changes in their markets or the wider environment, and that successful companies will constantly seek to innovate.

Change that does not alter the underlying strategy of an organisation is a description of convergent change, but is not something this specifically relevant to Peters' theory of Thriving on Chaos.

Leaders having a clear vision of what they want to achieve is one of the characteristics of leadership in change adept organisations, but again, is not specifically relevant to Peters' theory.

10.12 The correct answer is: Empowering others to act on the vision

The project team made up of the senior managers from across the company provides the guiding coalition to lead the project. The discussion the senior managers held with their departments allowed the vision to be communicated, and the announcement of bonuses is evidence of a quick win.

Empowering others to act on the vision involves getting rid of obstacles to change such as unhelpful structures or systems. In this case, LBP's IT system appears unable to support the online courses properly, and this has undermined the success of the new strategy.

10.13 The correct answers are:

- Willingness to stake personal results on results being achieved
- Self-confidence tempered with humility
- An ability to collaborate effectively

Kanter identified seven 'power skills' which change agents need in order to help them overcome resistance to change in organisations:

- An ability to collaborate effectively

- An ability to develop relationships based on trust and high ethical standards

- An ability to work independently and without relying on senior management to provide visible support. (**Note.** Kanter argues it is a power skill **not** to need visible support from management, meaning the option 'Visible support from senior management' is incorrect.)

- An ability to work across different business functions and business units

- Self-confidence, tempered with humility

- A willingness to stake personal rewards on results being achieved, and to take satisfaction from them achieving them

- Respecting the process of change, as well as the substance of the change

The options relating to best practices approaches based on prior experience and bringing a fresh perspective to a change initiative are examples of the advantages of using an external change agent to lead change, not power skills.

11 Strategic performance management

11.1 The correct answer is: Porter's Value Chain Analysis.

The Value Chain was based upon manufacturing companies, and will require extensive re-working of existing accounting information to be of commercial use. The Balanced Scorecard can be used by any business and may incorporate existing KPIs. Neither the BCG nor Ansoff's matrix require any accounting information to be input.

11.2 The correct answers are:

- Brand performance
- Quality of manufacturing

CSFs highlight the areas where a company must perform well in order to be successful, whereas KPIs are used to measure how well a company is performing in relation to its CSFs. To be successful JK will need to ensure the continuing quality of manufacturing and the strength of its brand. If this occurs then it should see increases in the measures (KPIs) of market share and customer satisfaction.

11.3 The correct answer is: Financial; customer; innovation and learning; internal business.

The four perspectives of the balanced scorecard are:

- Financial
- Customer
- Innovation and learning
- Internal business

11.4 The correct answer is: Financial.

The financial perspective is the highest level perspective, meaning that the measures and goals an organisation seeks to achieve in relation to the other three perspectives should, in turn, help an organisation to achieve its financial goals.

11.5 The correct answers are:

- Future strategic potential
- Present competitive position

These are assessments of a business's underlying position in relation to competitive forces and the stream of market opportunities.

The balanced scorecard's non-financial perspectives are the internal business perspective, the customer perspective and the innovation and learning perspective. These would include measures of office efficiency, customer satisfaction and intellectual assets and organisational learning respectively.

11.6 The correct answers are:

CSF	KPI	Target
Customer satisfaction	**Number of repeat customers**	**50% of shoppers return annually**
Growth in sales revenue	**Increase in market share**	**3% increase in like-for-like sales**

Customer satisfaction will relate to EAV's existing customers, and how satisfied they have been with their dealings with the company. If EAV is able to retain its existing customers this will suggest the customers are satisfied with the products and service they have received from EAV.

EAV's ability to increase its sales revenue will depend on its ability to attract new customers as well as to retain its existing ones. Increasing market share, and increasing sales, would both suggest it is doing this successfully.

11.7 The correct answers are:

- Awareness amongst performance car buyers of the superior performance of TRV's vehicles
- Annual reductions in the production costs of TRV's vehicles
- Superior performance of TRV's vehicles compared to its domestic and foreign rivals

The factors that will determine the profitability of TRV will be: customers' awareness of the vehicles' performance relative to competitors (because this can help to increase sales); reductions in cost (to preserve margins) and superior performance (to justify prices).

Superior comfort and reputation for CSR are likely to be of little interest to TRV's target customers.

11.8 The correct answer is: Innovation and learning.

One of the key aspects of the Innovation and learning perspective (also known as 'Learning and growth') is the number of new products developed.

The Customer perspective may also look at the proportion of sales from new products (to see how attractive new products are to customers) but new product development is most explicitly related to the Innovation and learning perspective.

11.9   The correct answer is: (i) and (iii) only.

The pyramid focuses on a range of objectives for both external effectiveness (related to customer satisfaction) and internal efficiency (related to flexibility and productivity).

The fact that the hierarchical nature of the pyramid encourages individual departments to link their operational goals to strategic goals is one of the strengths of the model.

However, one of the criticisms of the pyramid is that it tends to concentrate on two main groups of stakeholders only: shareholders and customers.

It does not look at measures which relate to other stakeholders, such as employees or suppliers.

11.10 The correct answers are:

- Ensure that senior managers welcome, and are seen to welcome, changes for the better.
- Understand people in the organisation and their needs.
- Recognise and encourage potential entrepreneurs.

The other two goals would not achieve their purpose; bureaucratic structures cause delays, not interactive feedback and innovation. Also switching to short-term horizons would discourage (rather than encourage) innovation, because the time delays between invention and commercial production/success can take a number of years.

11.11 The correct answers are:

A number of employees have said that they weren't sure what their objectives were, or what goals they were working towards:

Rewards

Employees have given up trying to reach their bonus targets because they feel they are neither achievable nor fair:

Standards

Customer satisfaction surveys have shown a decline in the reliability and responsiveness of the service customers have received from F's staff:

Dimensions

The dimensions building block is made up of results and determinants. The four determinants are: quality of service, flexibility, resource utilisation and innovation. The results of the customer satisfaction surveys suggest a decline in the quality of service.

Standards are the measures used to monitor an organisation's performance against each of the dimensions. However, in order for standards to be effective, employees must view them as fair and achievable, and must take ownership of them. The fact that the bonus targets are felt to be neither achievable nor fair suggests they are not working well as standards.

Rewards are the motivators which encourage employees to work towards the standards set. Effective rewards need to be clearly understood, should measure performance in areas the employees can control, and should motivate them to work towards the organisation's strategic objectives. However, in this case, the employees appear not to have a clear understanding of what the goals and objectives are.

12 Performance measurement

12.1   The correct answer is: Buying a rival to Division H, to acquire its market share of 6%.

G should not be sold due to its rapid growth potential. It is not far behind the market leader so investment may be warranted to make it a 'Star' product.

The smaller rival of H should be purchased to cement H's place as market leader, retaining its 'Star' product status.

F already has a dominant position in a mature market so it is a 'cash cow' which should be 'harvested'.

Whilst E has a small market share it appears to operate within a profitable niche and makes a substantial contribution to group profits. It should be retained.

12.2   The correct answers are:

- Long term forecasts of market trends
- Competitor prices and profit margins
- Assessments of potential acquisition targets

Strategic management accounting provides information that is more external and future orientated than traditional management accounting. As such it is more likely to report on long-term forecasts, competitors' performance and potential acquisition targets.

A traditional management accounts function would focus on internal flexed budgets and investment appraisals.

12.3   The correct answer is: Cost of capital is difficult to calculate.

RI reduces profit by a notional interest figure based on the investment level multiplied by the cost of capital.

As cost of capital is complex to calculate and is not a precise measure RI is often ignored.

One of the potential weaknesses of ROI is that it can encourage short term decision making and self-interest, which contradict the aims of goal congruence rather than supporting them.

Profit can be easily manipulated, but since it features in both RI and ROI calculations this has no bearing on the choice between the two.

The cost of capital can be amended to build in different levels of risk, which is one of the features that makes RI a superior measure.

12.4   The correct answers are:

- Differing legal frameworks in the different countries
- Different cultures
- Economic conditions in the different countries

Differing legal frameworks could impose different costs on the divisions – for example, regulations around minimum wages or health and safety.

Equally, the group will need to recognise the different cultures which are accepted in the different countries.

Differing economic conditions – for example, differences in inflation, or if one country is experiencing faster growth than another – make it harder to compare the performance of divisions in different countries.

Transfer pricing can actually be a useful measure of control in multinationals, for example, as a means of managing tax liabilities. Similarly, a decentralised structure could be appropriate for multinational groups because local managers could have a better understanding of their local markets, and the factors affecting performance in them.

12.5   The correct answer is: Profit is simple for managers to understand.

Profit is a measure that most non-financial managers can understand, which increases rather than reduces its popularity in business.

Profit can be manipulated by changing assumptions and accounting policies, making it less reliable as a performance measure.

Due to the narrow focus of profit, stakeholders such as customers are often omitted from consideration. Their interests can be accounted for by using a model such as the balanced scorecard.

By measuring profit only, expenditure on intangible assets such as training, marketing and R&D is discouraged. This can have an adverse effect on a company's long term prospects.

12.6 The correct answers are:

- The manager of Division B has an incentive to invest in the new machine which would be against the interest of shareholders

- The managerial bonus system is rewarding poor performance by the manager of Division B

- ROI is an unsuitable measure for evaluating new investments

The forecast ROI for the new machine means that the manager of A will reject the proposal as it lowers the ROI of the division, despite having a positive NPV and hence being in the best interests of shareholders. Conversely the manager of B will accept the proposal, despite the negative NPV, as the higher ROI will yield them a bonus. As such ROI is an unsuitable measure here as it leads to dysfunctional outcomes.

12.7 The correct answer is: Profit before interest and tax/Operations capital employed.

Profit is taken before tax (because tax is an appropriation of profit made from the use of investment); and before interest (because the inclusion of interest charges introduces the effect of financing decisions into a measurement of operating performance).

12.8 The correct answer is: Economic Value Added.

Economic Value Added (EVA) tries to overcome the problems of using accounting profits as the basis of performance measurement by using economic profit instead. One of the major differences between economic profit and accounting profit is that the former is adjusted for value building expenditures (such as development costs, advertising and promotions, and training) on the grounds that they will generate wealth for an organisation in future periods.

ROCE is a financial ratio that measures a company's profitability and the efficiency with which its capital is employed. Return on Capital Employed (ROCE) is calculated as: ROCE = Earnings Before Interest and Tax (EBIT) / Capital Employed.

Shareholder Value Analysis looks at the total return to the shareholders in terms of both dividends and share price growth. It is calculated as the present value of future free cash flows of the business, discounted at the weighted average cost of the capital of the business, less the market value of its debt.

Total shareholder return looks at the change in a company's share price for a given period, plus its free cash flow over the same period, as a percentage of the opening share price.

12.9 The correct answers are:

- Greater speed of decision making
- It improves the motivation of junior managers

While the other options may arise in a decentralised organisation, they are not necessarily features that are specifically associated with decentralisation.

12.10 The correct answers are:

- The range should be designed in a way which maximises its useful life

- Inventory levels as a percentage of sales revenue from the products should be kept as low as possible

- The operating profit margin the products earn should be maximised, either by increasing sales prices or by reducing costs

Shareholder value analysis focuses on seven 'value drivers' which drive the generation of cash in a business. These are: sales growth rate; operating profit margin; cash taxation rate; fixed capital investment rate; working capital investment rate; life of the business (or project); and cost of capital.

The 'Fixed capital investment rate' element of SVA relates to non-current assets as a percentage of sales revenue. The value drivers do not make any reference to intangible assets.

The adjustment to added back research and development costs is one of the adjustments required when calculating Economic Value Added (EVA), rather than SVA.

13 Mixed Bank 1

13.1 The correct answer is:

- A strategy that seeks to maintain relationships with governments, media, regulators and society at large to achieve sustainable advantage.

The non-market environment relates to the wider political environment in which an organisation operates. A firm's ability to worth with regulators and governments could potentially contribute to its competitive advantage, just as much as economic advantages it can develop over its rivals. Corporate political activity can be very important in the non-market environment.

13.2 The correct answer is:

- POOR: they did not understand the ethical principles involved correctly and the action they took was not strong enough in the circumstances.

The response is poor, because although some action is taken (ie the management accountant has expressed their concerns, and has recognised that ethics is a relevant factor) they have failed to demonstrate that they understand that their objectivity has also been compromised, thus failing to understand the ethical principles involved. Added to this, the management accountant has failed to take strong enough action to bring their manager's conflict of interest to anyone's attention within the firm.

13.3 The correct answer is: Legislative treaties and increased governmental risk.

The increased risk may be manifested in a variety of ways, such as taxation law, labour regulation and economic policy on such matters as ownership.

13.4 The correct answer is: (1), (2) and (3) only.

A high contribution per unit of limiting factor, potential damage to the production or sale of complementary products, and strategic value of staying in the market are all key considerations. Fixed overheads are not relevant for decision-making and should be excluded unless they are specifically associated with the product.

13.5 The correct answer is: Related vertical backward diversification.

It is related to their current business (hence this is 'related' rather than 'unrelated' diversification) and the company being acquired is a supplier to the company acquiring it. Therefore the acquisition represents a move backwards (or upstream) through the supply chain.

13.6 The correct answers are:

Information systems determine corporate/business strategy	**False**
Information systems support corporate/business strategy	**True**

Although IS/IT do not determine business strategy, they can help support corporate / business strategy. For example, IS/IT may provide a possible source of competitive advantage by using new technology not yet available to competitors, or using existing technology in a different way.

IS/IT may also help in the formulation of business strategy by providing information from internal and external sources.

13.7 The correct answer is: Falling profits are the effect of increased power of substitutes.

Demand for renting movies has fallen because people can download and watch movies online instead. Watching movies online therefore provides a substitute for renting movies. The key point about substitutes is that they are goods or services from another industry which satisfy the same customer needs. By extension, therefore, new entrants (such as WXY) are entering a different industry to that which TUV is operating in.

13.8   The correct answer is: Provide and sell a motive or reason to change.

This describes the 'Unfreeze' stage of Lewin's model.

13.9   The correct answer is: The team needs to buy into, or have ownership of, a decision, plan or strategic change.

Democratic leadership encourages members of the team to participate in the decision-making process. In turn, this can promote better contributions from the group and increased morale. Moreover, team members will be more committed to the success of a new initiative if they have helped to develop it.

Where a team needs a new vision, is subject to rapid change, or is a crisis there is no time for deliberation, therefore more autocratic styles of management are required.

13.10   The correct answer is: Innovation and learning

The perspectives represented by each of the KPIs, in turn, are:

1 – Internal business, as average time between a patient arriving and being seen by a member of medical staff looks at efficiency
2 – Financial, as this is a cost measure
3 – Internal business, as it looks at the accuracy of internal processes
4 – Customer, as it looks at customer satisfaction

The missing perspective is therefore Innovation and learning.

14 Mixed Bank 2

14.1   The correct answers are:

- Management has a high degree of comfort with the techniques of the rational approach.
- The future can be forecast with reasonable certainty.
- In an organisation where departmental loyalties take priority over attaining corporate goals.

The first option is incorrect as the rational model is a **long term** planning tool. The fourth option is wrong as the rational model inhibits innovation, as it places a premium on planning rather than inspiration.

14.2   The correct answer is:

- The use of its equipment by hospitals to enhance appearance as well as to assist in curing illness and injury.

Three of the options given here are ethically very questionable: charging higher prices to countries least able to afford them; inaccurate diagnosis leading to patient harm; and poor pay and working conditions to both staff, and in the supply chain.

Although enhancing appearance is non-critical, it is still providing a benefit to the people who receive it, whereas the situations being described in the other three options are detrimental to the groups affected by them.

14.3   The correct answer is: The option to abandon a project.

If revenue streams from the project are highly uncertain, the option to abandon the project if things go wrong is valuable. This is particularly important for projects involving new products where their acceptance by the market is uncertain.

14.4 The correct answers are:

- It can provide an early warning of future problems
- It may generate new ideas from which all participants benefit;
- It focuses on improvement in key areas and sets targets, which are challenging but 'achievable'.

What is really achievable can be discovered by examining what others have achieved: managers are thus able to accept that they are not being asked to perform miracles.

Both of the other statements are incorrect; benchmarking does not have to be carried out by external consultants, and while it can identify areas where performance can be improved, there is no guarantee that it will improve performance in these areas.

14.5 The correct answer is: 29.4%

Current present value

Year		Cash flow $000	Discount factor $000	Discounted cash flows $000
0	Investment	(20,000)	1.000	(20,000)
1-3	Net cash flows	11,000	2.577	28,347
				8,347

Therefore net cash flows must reduce by 8,347/28,347 = 29.4%

Alternative working

Annual net flows at breakeven = 20,000/2.577 = $7,761

Reduction in sales receipts = 11,000 – 7,761/11,000 = 29.4%

14.6 The correct answers are:

- An organisation's IT costs escalate.
- Systems may not be integrated.
- Poor quality information is produced.

If there is no IT strategy, piecemeal investment in IT may take place and the costs can escalate. Systems will be developed on an ad hoc basis and so may not be easily integrated. The quality of the information produced is likely to be inferior.

By having an IT strategy in place, the systems that are developed are likely to be business-led and IT can be exploited to gain competitive advantage.

14.7 The correct answer is: A virtual organisation.

A virtual organisation is a collection of geographically dispersed groups or organisations that depend on electronic linking (such as B's EDI system) in order to complete the production process.

14.8 The correct answer is: Rescoping.

This sounds like it could be a plausible stage for the start of the process, however, the correct R to describe this stage is reframing.

The 4 Rs, in sequence, are: Reframing, Restructuring, Revitalising, and Renewal.

14.9 The correct answers are:

- Communicate a vision
- Energise teams
- Support the change process

NE initiated the change when he laid down the guiding principles. However, the fact that managers and staff didn't know whether their ideas were appropriate suggests that NE has not communicated his vision effectively to them.

The fact that staff don't have sufficient resources to implement any plans they have suggests they have not been given the support they need to implement the changes effectively; and their discouragement with the project (after only a few months) suggests NE has failed to energise them (for example, through achieving some quick -wins and thereby reinforcing that the initiative has the potential to be successful).

14.10 The correct answers are:

- Equitable
- Achievable
- Owned

Fitzgerald & Moon developed the Building Block Model consisting of three core elements of performance measurement: Standards, Dimensions and Rewards. Standards should be equitable, achievable and owned. Dimensions include Results (financial and competitive performance) and Determinants (quality, flexibility, innovation and resource utilisation). Rewards should be motivational, clear and controllable.

15 Mixed Bank 3

15.1 The correct answer is: The role of a Company Director combines some of the role of film producers with some of the role of film directors.

The Directors of a company are responsible for taking strategic decisions and ensuring that the resulting strategies are properly implemented (which corresponds, in part, to the role of the film director).

The Board of Directors in a company also has a responsibility for ensuring that a satisfactory dialogue takes place with shareholders (which corresponds, in part, to the role of the film producer.)

15.2 The correct answers are:

- The removal of positional authority in the group to enable free discussion to take place.
- The independence of members enables unpopular or novel ideas to be discussed.
- Its group nature facilitates the sharing of knowledge and encourages a shared view.

The first option is incorrect as it talks about probabilities, which contradicts the statement in the question about not relying on statistical methods.

The second statement is also incorrect because it is unlikely that staff across all levels of the organisation would be invited to a meeting – the meeting attendees would be invited more selectively. This second statement would be more appropriate for describing a brainstorming session.

15.3 The correct answer is: Delphi technique.

The Delphi technique involves a number of experts independently and anonymously giving their opinions and insights on a particular trend and how it may develop. Initial results are summarised and the summary is returned to the experts, who are then asked to respond again. The process is repeated until a consensus is achieved.

15.4 The correct answer is: Procurement.

Inbound logistics; marketing and sales; and service are all primary activities.

The support activities in Porter's value chain are: infrastructure; HRM; technology development; and procurement.

15.5 The correct answer is: (1) and (2) only.

An increase in price sensitivity is likely to reduce sales of a differentiated product as customers migrate to the cost leader's (probably) cheaper offering.

Marketing communication is fundamental to a strategy of differentiation, since prospective customers must appreciate why the product is different if they are to be motivated to buy it.

The cost leader is selling to its own market segment and is unlikely to be concerned with the market for the differentiated product.

A unique feature protected by patent will make differentiation more effective as a marketing tool, since competitors will be unable to copy it.

15.6 The correct answers are:

- The success of business depends on the quality of the information in the organisation.
- IT can provide the organisation with the competitive advantage needed for commercial success.

An organisation needs an IT strategy because IT can provide the competitive advantage needed for commercial success. Unless the organisation has a strategy it may miss these opportunities.

The success of business depends on the quality of the information, because the information provides the basis for decisions which are made by the organisation. The IT systems provide this information.

If IT is left to the technical department, the decisions made may not be business-led and so may not be appropriate. IT permeates the whole organisation and will often affect everyone and so it is important that senior management time is spent on it. The total expenditure on IT can be great and so strategic direction is needed.

15.7 The correct answers are:

- Reduction in the transactions costs of dealing with suppliers.

- Higher production and sales due to suppliers responding quickly to demand and leading to fewer stock outs of components.

- Lower inventory holding costs because the reduced cost of placing and processing orders means AAA can place orders more frequently.

Cost reduction, quicker ordering and reduced inventory levels and all benefits of e-procurement. In theory, e-procurement can also lead to a wider choice of suppliers, through the use of e-sourcing to find new suppliers from around the world. However, AAA's intention to build partnerships with its suppliers means that it is unlikely to be constantly shopping around to find new suppliers; so, in this case, the second option is not correct.

E-procurement enables anyone to order goods from anywhere, but this facility also means that the risk of unauthorised purchases being made increases.

15.8 The correct answers are:

- Education and communication
- Participation and involvement
- Negotiation and agreement

Kotter and Schlesinger identify six methods of dealing with resistance to change:

- Education and communication
- Participation and involvement
- Facilitation and support
- Negotiation and agreement
- Manipulation and co-optation
- Coercion

Therefore neither 'networking and support', nor 'mutual co-operation' are correct.

15.9 The correct answers are:

- An effective team has a unity of purpose and all team members understand this purpose.
- An effective team involves its stakeholders in assessing progress towards goals.

It is not true to say that teams always need a democratic leader – the leadership style should change given the needs of the team; for example, autocratic styles may work better in a crisis. It is also not true to say teams should avoid conflict; indeed managed conflict can lead to innovation; a hallmark of successful teams.

15.10 The correct answer is: Quality of service.

Quality of service looks at matters like reliability, responsiveness, courtesy, competence and availability. It can be measured through customer satisfaction surveys.

Resource utilisation considers how efficiently resources are being used, either human resources (labour) or buildings and equipment etc.

In the 'Results and Determinants' framework, 'Competitive performance' and 'Financial performance' are results rather than determinants.

16 Mixed Bank 4

16.1 The correct answers are:

- Evaluation of the competitors' actions
- Evaluation of forecast passenger volumes
- Evaluation of public concern for environmental damage

Strategic analysis is long-term, company-wide analysis undertaken at a high level. The options referring to staff recruitment, and which planes to use, are of a more operational nature eg lower-level, short-term and more localised decisions.

16.2 The correct answer is: The mission gives managers a focus for setting objectives.

The mission statement gives the purpose and strategy of the organisation. The company will then use this as a focus for setting appropriate objectives.

16.3 The correct answer is: (i) only

Game theory highlights that both competition and co-operation can exist in an industry, and it highlights the importance of competitor analysis and having an insight into competitors' strategies.

However, critics of game theory argue that it does **not** provide any useful guidance about how to actually *implement* whatever co-operative strategies an organisation may develop in conjunction with competitors.

16.4   The correct answer is: Both (1) and (2).

A balanced portfolio is necessary to ensure funds to support newer products with long term potential. Cash cows are typically the sources of the funds required to support and develop question marks.

16.5   The correct answers are:

- Local culture
- Quality of local employees
- Appropriate management style

The remaining options need to be considered by a global organisation moving into a new country, but not specifically in relation to human resource management.

16.6   The correct answers are:

- Consider how IT can support business objectives.
- Define business objectives.

As part of dealing with the organisation's current use of IT you need to identify gaps in system coverage and assess how good the current systems are, both technically and in terms of value to the business. Identifying potential opportunities and threats that IT can bring requires the use of creative thinking.

16.7   The correct answers are:

- Long-term contracts allow much greater certainty in planning for the future.
- An outsourcing company has economies of scale.
- New skills and knowledge become available.

Unfortunately, outsourcing does not allow increased managerial control nor does it transfer the information system implementation process to users. These are both advantages associated with user-developed systems, which would be an alternative way for developing the new information system.

16.8   The correct answers are:

- Initiatives introduced by a new CEO who has just joined the organisation
- A new organisational structure which leads to new job responsibilities
- The implementation of a new IT system.

Internal triggers are internal to the organisation itself, whereas external triggers come from the outside world.

Although the CEO may have joined from the organisation from outside, he or she will then be employed by the organisation. So any changes he or she introduces will be within the organisation only.

Equally, the new organisation structure and the new IT system will only affect the organisation.

16.9   The correct answer is: Education and communication.

Education and communication is an approach based on persuasion. The reasons for the change and the means by which it will be achieved are explained in detail.

16.10   The correct answer is: Translating the vision, Communicating and linking, Business planning, Feedback and learning.

The four stage sequence which Kaplan and Norton recommend is:

Translating the vision: the organisation's mission must be expressed in a way that has clear operational meaning for each employee.

Communicating and linking: the vision or mission must be linked to departmental and individual objectives, including those that transcend traditional short-term financial goals.

Business planning: the scorecard is used to prioritise objectives and allocate resources in order to make the best progress towards strategic goals.

Feedback and learning: the organisation learns to use feedback on performance to promote progress against all four perspectives.

17 Mixed Bank 5

17.1   The correct answers are:

Traditional approach	**Position-based**
New CEO's approach	**Resource-based**

Organisations adopting a position-based approach to strategy analyse their environments (for example through PEST analysis and Porter's five forces) before setting their objectives and strategy, and they try to ensure that their strategic plans provide a good 'fit' with their environments.

By contrast, organisations pursuing a resource-based approach focus on their own competences and capabilities, rather than trying to design a strategy which 'fits' with the environment.

Accounting-led approaches to strategy start by focusing on an organisation's key stakeholders and their objectives, and then look to develop plans designed to achieve those objectives. There is no reference in the scenario to X's stakeholders and their objectives, so this approach is not relevant here.

17.2   The correct answer is: Organisations exist for the benefit of shareholders.

The traditional view of social responsibility argues that companies only exist for the benefit of their shareholders, and therefore it rejects the ideas that the needs and opinions of other, wider groups of stakeholders should be taken into account.

A more progressive view, sometimes referred to as the ecology model, recognises that the needs and opinions of all stakeholder groups (both financial and non financial) are valid.

The ecology model recognises that organisations exist within a wider environment and that there are many advantages to be gained from recognising the needs of a wide range of stakeholders

17.3   The correct answer is: Relevance.

Information should often be accurate where possible, but total accuracy is not always possible, especially, for example, in the case of forecasting information.

Information should often be brief and concise, but there are times when detail is needed - for example, think about legal information and the lengthy detail that solicitors often need to draw up contracts.

Good quality information must be timely which means that it ought to be available in time for when it is needed. This doesn't necessarily mean that it has to be produced quickly though. Making speed a quality of good information may be to the detriment of other characteristics.

Relevance is the only characteristic listed which should not be compromised – the information being produced needs to meet the needs of the recipients and users of that information.

17.4   The correct answer is: High relative market share, low industry growth rate.

This combination typically provides good revenues and requires only moderate marketing costs.

It is important to remember that the BCG matrix refers to relative, not absolute, market share.

The market leader may have a low absolute market share in a highly competitive industry with many players, but it will have a high (>1) share relative to its largest competitor.

17.5   The correct answer is: (i) only

Franchising allows a business to expand using less capital than if it grows organically.

Firms often franchise because they cannot readily raise the capital required to set up company-owned stores.

However, one of the potential risks of franchising is that poor performance by individual franchisees could harm the overall brand.

17.6 The correct answers are:

- The speed of processing is improved.
- The cost of a computer system is lower than the manual system it replaces, mainly because the jobs previously performed by human operators are now done by computers.
- The accuracy of data/information and processing is improved, because a computer does not make mistakes.

Three examples of efficiency are: firstly, the speed of processing is improved eg, response times in satisfying customer orders are improved; secondly, the cost of a computer system is lower than the manual system it replaces, mainly because computers now do the jobs previously performed by human operators. The third example is that the accuracy of data/information and processing is improved, because a computer does not make mistakes.

Effectiveness focuses primarily on the relationship of the organisation with its environment. An example is where automation is pursued because it is expected the company will be more effective at increasing market share or satisfying customer needs. Another example is where front office systems are developed to improve the organisation's decision-making capability to improve the effectiveness of the organisation.

17.7 The correct answer is: A focus on supplying customer needs.

A marketing orientation involves structuring an organisation's activities around the needs of its customers.

17.8 The correct answers are:

- Reduction in the legal age for drinking.
- Increase in average household disposable income.
- Tightening of border controls reducing illegal imports.

These will all lead to an increase in legitimate sales. Changes in taste from draught to bottled beers will change the product sales mix but not necessarily change overall sales. The remaining options would tend to reduce demand for alcoholic drinks, and therefore reduce the brewery's sales.

17.9 The correct answer is: It may need to be imposed on an organisation in a crisis situation.

Change which is imposed on an organisation is top down change. A top down change may need to be imposed on an organisation in a crisis or turnaround situation, but the potential danger of imposing change on staff is that they resist or resent it. (This is, therefore, a potential disadvantage of top down change, not bottom up change.)

By contrast, the responsibility for bottom up change does not rest solely with senior management. Staff are involved in contributing to ideas in the changes, but this may make bottom up change a slower process to implement, and a harder process to control, than top down change.

17.10 The correct answer is: NPV of future cash flows discounted at the cost of capital.

Shareholder value analysis is a method of estimating the economic value of an investment by examining discounted cash flows.

Cash flows are considered more reliable than profit as they cannot be so easily manipulated.

Adjusting profit for elements such as R&D gives economic value added.

18 Mixed Bank 6

18.1   The correct answer is: Tangible resources.

C plc is gearing its strategy around tangible resources, as these refer to the physical assets of an organisation, such as plant, labour and finance. In this instance it is new plant and machinery.

Strategic capability is the adequacy and suitability of the resources and competences of an organisation for it to survive and prosper. Competences are the activities and processes through which an organisation deploys its resources effectively. Intangible resources are non-physical assets such as information, reputation and knowledge.

18.2   The correct answers are:

- Shareholders – want a return on their investment.
- Suppliers – will expect to be paid and will be interested in the future.
- Customers – want products and services.

Government is an external stakeholder, with an interest in taxation and compliance with the law. Employees are internal stakeholders since they are part of the organisation.

Note that internal and connected stakeholders are sometimes grouped together as primary stakeholders in that they have a contractual relationship with the organisation. In this analysis, external stakeholders are known as secondary stakeholders.

18.3   The correct answer is: Real options.

Real options will allow PPI plc to value any follow-on investments in shale gas extraction, as well as the value of having the option to abandon or delay investment. Delphi technique would ask a panel of anonymous experts for their opinions on a trend and how it might develop; scenario planning might deliver a range of possible financial outcomes, and regression analysis may allow for extrapolation. However none of these latter techniques will specifically address the financial impact of any potential gas extractions that PPI might be able to make in the future.

18.4   The correct answers are:

- Management Information Systems
- Materials

Speedies has identified weaknesses in its management accounts (ie Management Information Systems) and its supplier relations (Materials). Make-up refers to internal structures and culture; Markets refers to customer relations, and Methods relates to how the company manufactures its products.

18.5   The correct answer is: Increased risk of focusing on a single market.

The risk is spread across several geographical markets following globalisation (so this is an advantage of globalisation). The remaining options are all possible drawbacks of globalisation.

18.6   The correct answers are:

Director of IT	**Business led**
Team members	**Infrastructure led**

The business led approach is the top-down approach, advocated by the Director of IT. A business led approach focuses on the way IS/IT can support business objectives.

The infrastructure led approach is driven from the bottom up, and involves systems users and experts, as advocated by the team members.

The Mixed approach is not mentioned in the scenario. This is more of an innovative approach often involving entrepreneurs and visionary thinkers who identify innovative ways of using existing IS/IT.

18.7 The correct answer is: It is a simple exercise.

Practical customer profitability calculations can be complex or rely on estimates. Assigning indirect costs to different activities or customers is often difficult.

18.8 The correct answer is: Adaptation.

Balogun and Hope Hailey classify change style by comparing the scope of change (realignment or transformation) and nature of change (incremental or 'big bang'). In this case the change is gradual (incremental) and doesn't change the paradigm (realignment) – hence the type of change is Adaptation.

Reconstruction involves a more rapid change response within the same paradigm, often as a result of increased competition. Evolution involves a gradual shift but leads to a new paradigm, often as a result of planned change. Revolution involves fast-paced and wide-ranging change, often to ensure an organisation's survival in response to extreme environmental changes.

18.9 The correct answers are:

- Support for positive behaviour and confrontation of negative behaviour
- Communication of desired norms
- Recruitment and selection of the right people

To establish new norms needs time, persuasion and commitment; norms cannot be forced upon people, and getting rid of people who do not willingly take to the changes will cause much resentment throughout the organisation.

Cultural change will involve letting people know what the desired norms are, supporting positive behaviour and confronting negative behaviour. It is also likely to involve recruiting and selecting the type of person with the relevant beliefs and attitudes for the desired new culture.

18.10 The correct answer is: Interest rate expectations for future borrowing.

As investment levels are similar for both types of attraction, the cost of borrowing and repayments will be similar for both and therefore not very useful when making the investment decision.

19 Mixed Bank 7

19.1 The correct answer is: (ii) only.

Part of the strategic analysis stage of the rational model is an environmental analysis – identifying the opportunities and threats in an environment. However, one of the perceived problems of the rational model approach to strategic planning is that its rigidity prevents companies from responding quickly to unforeseen opportunities or threats, or other changes.

19.2 The correct answers are:

- To generate strategies for the company.
- To determine operational priorities.
- To control the company.

Objectives are vital for strategic management in an organisation. Strategies are developed to achieve objectives. As objectives cascade down the organisation, they can be used to set lower level targets, thus determining operational priorities. The control process begins with an assessment of current performance against objectives.

Consideration of stakeholders' interests and priorities may be used in setting objectives; objectives will be derived from a mission statement.

19.3 The correct answer is: Game theory.

Game theory illustrates the way that strategic interactions between competitors can produce outcomes that were not intended by any of the players.

19.4 The correct answers are:

- Problem solving
- Choice between solutions
- Solution implementation

Stabell and Fjeldstad identified five primary activities in their Value Shop theory. These were:

Problem-finding and acquisition: Recording, reviewing and formulating the problem to be solved, and choosing an overall approach to solving the problem. Marketing effort could be required here as well as professional expertise.

Problem solving: more extensive professional expertise must be deployed to identify and evaluate potential solutions to the issue at hand.

Choice between solutions: A preferred solution is chosen (in consultation with the client) from the alternative solutions which have been identified.

Solution implementation: This activity involves communicating, organising and implementing the chosen solution.

Control and feedback: Measuring and evaluating the extent to which the solution has solved the initial problem, to ensure the effectiveness of the solution.

19.5 The correct answer is: Selling wooden flooring in the existing store.

Product development means selling a new product into an existing market. Opening a new store in the next town involves a new market: this is market development (current product, new market).

Selling wooden flooring in a new store is diversification (new product, new market).

Increasing warehouse space is not a product-market vector event.

19.6 The correct answer is: Strategic.

Peppard's applications portfolio classifies each program / system that a business operates according to its strategic importance in the current competitive environment and the predicted future competitive environment. In the scenario, it is clear the ERP system is currently of high importance, and the levels of continual investment indicate it will continue to be important in the future, making it a 'Strategic' application.

19.7 The correct answer is: Transaction marketing focuses on a single sales transaction at a time.

Transaction marketing focuses on single sales rather than trying to develop customer relationships.

Transaction marketing focuses on product features, while relationship marketing focuses on customer benefits.

19.8 The correct answers are:

New Vice Chancellor	**Driving force**
Lobbying group	**Driving force**
Government policy	**Restraining force**
Current private donors	**Restraining force**
STI staff	**Restraining force**

The new Vice Chancellor has been appointed to drive change, and to this end has joined the lobbying group whose aim is to effect a change in Government policy.

Factors opposing change are: the Government policy statement that no extra funds will be available; the current levels of private donations which are harming the financial position of STI; and the staff who are threatening strike action against the cost-cutting wage freeze policy.

19.9   The correct answer is: Evolution.

Evolution is an incremental process that leads to a new paradigm.

Adaptation is an incremental process, but does not require the development of a new paradigm.

Reconstruction can also be undertaken within an existing paradigm, but it requires rapid and extensive action (not incremental change).

Transformation is one of the headings on the 'Scope of change' axis on the matrix (Realignment is the other).

19.10   The correct answer is: Commerciality.

The method of transfer pricing should meet three criteria:

Equity (provides a fair measure of divisional performance)
Neutrality (avoids the distortion of business decision making)
Administrative simplicity

20 Mixed Bank 8

20.1   The correct answers are:

- Know the business
- Manage patterns
- Reconcile change and continuity

Mintzberg identified five essential activities in strategic management. These are:

Managing **stability** (not 'instability' as shown in the question)

Detecting **discontinuity**. Environments do not change regularly, nor are they always turbulent. Some changes are more important than others.

Know the business. This has to include an awareness and understanding of operations.

Manage patterns. Detect emerging patterns and help them take shape if appropriate.

Reconcile change and continuity. Avoid concentrating on one or the other.

20.2   The correct answer is: Congruence.

If objectives are not congruent, dysfunctional behaviour will arise and the goals of the organisation will not be achieved. In order that individuals are clear as to what is required objectives are set in accordance with the SMART mnemonic.

20.3   The correct answers are:

A quantitative technique to check any underlying correlations between two variables	**Regression analysis**
An expected future trend pattern obtained by extrapolation. It is principally concerned with quantitative factors, rather than accounting for personal judgements	**Projection**
A prediction of future events and their quantification for planning purposes	**Forecast**

20.4   The correct answer is: Question mark.

The BCG matrix assesses portfolio holdings via relative market share (own share / largest competitor's share, where >1 is high and < 1 is low) and market growth (above or below 10% per annum). In this scenario, Sarger has 'low' relative market share (as it is smaller than 'Retirement breaks') but it is operating in an industry where growth is 'high'. Therefore, from Giga's perspective, Sarger is a 'Question mark'.

BPP
LEARNING MEDIA

20.5   The correct answer is: Management buy out.

A management buy out is the purchase of a business from its existing owners by members of the existing management team, generally in association with a financing institution.

A management buy in is similar to a management buy out, but the new management team comes from outside the current business, rather than being the members of the existing management team.

20.6   The correct answers are:

Management Information System (MIS)	**(E)** – Converts data from mainly internal sources into report formats.
Decision Support System (DSS)	**(B)** – Uses data and data analysis tools to support semi-structured choices.
Enterprise Resource Planning System (ERPS)	**(D)** – Stores and integrates data from a range of operating systems across all business units.
Executive Information System (EIS)	**(C)** – Delivers high level outputs, using data from internal and external sources and using and historic, current and future information.
Transaction Processing System (TPS)	**(A)** – Processes large volumes of data via real time or batch processes.

20.7   The correct answers are:

- The level of competitiveness within the market is high.
- The company has limited resources.

If demand for the product is greater than supply or the product is unique, the product is likely to succeed whether the company segments the market or not.

20.8   The correct answer is: Cultural Web.

The Cultural Web looks at a range of factors including Symbols and Organisational Structure, as well as Stories, Controls, Power Structures, Routines and Rituals and the overall Paradigm (the assumptions and beliefs held by the organisation's decision makers). Whilst structure also features within the 7S model, symbols do not. Hofstede looked at aspects of national cultures and Schein discusses the artefacts, values and assumptions that make up organisational culture.

20.9   The correct answer is: The organisation's product.

The specifications of the product itself are determined by other market and production factors. However, it is worth adding that the product can affect the culture indirectly. If, for reasons of market positioning, the product is improved, the changes will contribute to a culture where employees identify with the quality image of the product.

Staff selection, reward policies and management style are the obvious tools of cultural change: getting only the right sort of people into the organisation, encouraging only desirable behaviour and attitudes, and selling the values of the organisation.

20.10 The correct answers are:

- There is greater awareness of local problems by decision makers.
- There is greater speed of decision-making and faster response to changing events.

The organisation can have greater speed of decision-making and response to changing events because there is no need to refer decisions upwards. This is particularly important in rapidly changing markets.

Pro-centralisation arguments stress that because decisions are made centrally, they are easy to co-ordinate. Also, a flatter structure reduces overhead costs; but decentralisation could increase management costs because managers will be required for each local business unit.

Finally, centralisation, rather than decentralisation, will mean that procedures and documentation can more easily be standardised across the organisation.

Notes